A PLUME BOOK

SAVED BY CAKE

MARIAN KEYES is the international bestselling author of *Watermelon, Lucy Sullivan Is Getting Married, Rachel's Holiday, Last Chance Saloon, Sushi for Beginners, Angels, The Other Side of the Story, Anybody Out There, This Charming Man,* and *The Brightest Star in the Sky.* Her two collections of journalism, *Under the Duvet* and *Further Under the Duvet,* are also available from Penguin. Marian lives in Dublin with her husband.

There's more Marian at www.mariankeyes.com.

Marian Keyes
Saved by Cake

photography by Alistair Richardson

A PLUME BOOK

PLUME
Published by the Penguin Group
Penguin Group (USA) Inc., 375 Hudson Street
New York, New York 10014, USA

USA | Canada | UK | Ireland | Australia | New Zealand | India | South Africa | China
Penguin Books Ltd, Registered Offices: 80 Strand, London WC2R 0RL, England
For more information about the Penguin Group visit penguin.com

Originally published in Great Britain by Michael Joseph, an imprint of Penguin Books Ltd.
Published by Plume, a member of Penguin Group (USA) Inc., 2013

LIBRARY OF CONGRESS CATALOGING-IN-PUBLICATION DATA
has been applied for.

Printed in the United States of America
1   3   5   7   9   10   8   6   4   2

PUBLISHER'S NOTE
The recipes contained in this book are to be followed exactly as written. The Publisher is not responsible
for your specific health or allergy needs that may require medical supervision. The Publisher is not
responsible for any adverse reactions to the recipes contained in this book.

ALWAYS LEARNING   PEARSON

Contents

For Himself, with all my love

Introduction

Medically speaking, there is no such thing as a nervous breakdown. Which is very annoying to discover when you're right in the middle of one.

Mind you, I didn't know I was having one until I was about 6 months into it. It started in October 2009, when panic started rolling up from my gut and down from my head and pushing out from behind my eyes. I felt like I was dreaming, like I'd woken up in the middle of a horrible nightmare, only to discover that I'd been awake all along. Too much reality was rushing in through my eyes. I felt desperate and terrified without knowing why, while I was afraid to tell anyone how I felt because I knew they'd tell me there was nothing to be afraid of and I knew that that wouldn't make the fear go away. I put all my energy into acting "normal," but I felt like I was driving a car where the controls were no longer working. Crowds terrified me, people zoomed at me, their words rained down on me like electric sparks, and my mouth wouldn't work to produce the right response.

I was in the middle of promoting a novel and I thought it must be the stress of that, perhaps an overload of adrenaline, but when the book promotion came to an end, I plunged far deeper into the awful, alien strangeness. It was time for me to start writing again—I'd started a book a couple of months before and it was waiting for me to continue with it—but I didn't know how. I couldn't manage to make an off-the-cuff remark about the weather, never mind write a novel.

I went away on holiday, to a beautiful tropical place, and at the risk of sounding disgustingly ungrateful, I felt like I was in hell. The sea, the sky, the sun, it all looked sinister and strange. I was afraid to be anywhere. I desperately wanted to go home. Even when I was at home. I hardly recognized where I lived. I barely recognized my husband, my mother, my own face. I wondered if I was dead—if I'd accidentally managed to die without noticing it—and was in hell.

I was diagnosed with depression, but it didn't feel like depression. Granted, I had lots of the symptoms: I couldn't sleep; I couldn't breathe; I couldn't eat; I couldn't read—by the time I came to the end of a sentence, I'd forgotten the start. Time had slowed down and each second took an eternity to tick by. Everything looked ugly and pointy and scary, even babies and flowers and Mulberry bags.

But I didn't feel depressed; what I felt was very, very afraid. I felt like I'd been poisoned, like my brain had been poisoned. I felt like there had been an avalanche in my head and I'd been shunted along by some awful force, to some strange place, off the map, where there was nothing I recognized and no one familiar. I was totally lost.

Some people will look at the outside of my life and see that I want for nothing and say that I'm just feeling sorry for myself, and that's their prerogative. Some people don't understand and will never understand, and I envy them. But the brain or the psyche or whatever we should call it is a delicate and difficult-to-understand thing. Whatever was—is—happening to me has nothing to do with my circumstances.

The best way to describe it is I feel like I'm in a science-fiction movie. I feel like I'm living in a parallel universe. I'm on a planet that looks very similar to Earth, but it pulses with a totally different energy, something malign and threatening. The people I know and love have been replaced with sinister doppelgängers and I feel like I'll never get back home. The way back has closed and disappeared and I'm trapped here in this awful, unfamiliar place.

I've tried curing myself in countless different ways. I took—take—a variety of antidepressants, I spent time in a psychiatric hospital—I thought it might be a sanctuary, literally an asylum—but everywhere I went, I took myself with me. I've tried Cognitive Behavioral Therapy, acupuncture, reiki, meditation, mindfulness, B_{12} injections, Bach Flower Remedies, journaling, ice-cold showers—anything that was recommended, I gave it a go. I tried exercising, but it seemed such a brutal thing to do to my terribly fragile self. I tried yoga, but I couldn't be alone in my own head. I tried spending time with friends, but that terrified me because I didn't recognize them. I tried focusing on other people, on any way I could help, but got knocked back at every attempt—I tried to volunteer for various charities, but was defeated by their complicated, lengthy application forms. I went to donate blood and they told me to hop it because I'd lived in the UK during the mad cow drama. I asked if anyone needed their living room painted, but no one did.

I begged people to let me drive them places. Driving was the one skill I could still manage. I knew I was disconnected from the world, so I drove with extra care. Sometimes I stopped at bus stops and offered to take people wherever they wanted to go, but no one would ever get in with me. Not—I think—because they saw I was mad, but because no one gets into cars with strangers.

Friends and family allowed me to give them lifts and I thanked them over and over. My previous self never had enough time to do such things; now I had endless, endless days and hours and minutes to fill. The old me used to speed up at yellow lights; now I slowed down, grateful to legitimately kill a few seconds at a red light. I kept trying to write. I made a contract with myself that I'd do an hour a day, even if I just sat in front of the computer and stared at the screen, but I couldn't manage even that.

I thought a lot about dying. I had a "suicide bag" that included, among other things, sheets of letter-size paper, Scotch tape, and big markers. These were to write big warning signs to be stuck to the door of the hotel bathroom, warning the chambermaid not to come in. I didn't want her traumatized. "STOP!" The notes said. "DON'T COME IN! I HAVE KILLED MYSELF. CALL THE GUARDS." (I'd decided, after lots of deliberating, that it would be better to kill myself at a hotel. I even had the right one picked out—a grim concrete block. I'd always thought it was the sort of place you'd go to if you wanted to kill yourself. I felt that if I did it at home, the house would be poisoned forever for Himself. That's the kind of logic my brain was presenting myself with.)

But though I hovered—and still hover—on the brink of suicide, I did feel enough of a sense of responsibility to the people who loved me not to go through with it. Whatever was going on with me, I had to wait it out. I had to find ways of passing the time until I was restored to myself again.

Then, one day, my friend Helen Cosgrove was visiting. Her birthday was coming up and all of a sudden I decided I wanted to bake Helen a birthday cake. I hadn't baked in decades, not since myself and my classmates had been forced to assemble some joyless rock cakes in Home Economics when we were thirteen. To be honest, I didn't really hold with baking. I was suspicious of anything "crafty." The resurgence in knitting and needlepoint and suchlike, I thought it was a bit of an affectation. And who had the time to bake? Why would you spend time and effort making something yourself when you could just go out and buy something far nicer in Marks & Spencers? I'd secretly mocked any person who had ever engaged with a piping bag.

But things were different now. So I baked Helen a cake—a chocolate cheesecake, as it happens. And I enjoyed making it so much that I baked another. And another. I started reading recipe books and looking up stuff on the Internet. I investigated the science of baking and I went to a couple of courses (nothing too challenging, but enough for me to get the basics).

I couldn't stop baking. And although I consumed a truly heroic quantity of my results, I couldn't eat it all and eventually had to start giving it away—to family members, neighbors, random strangers. At first people were charmed. Then a little overwhelmed. Eventually when they saw me coming, baked goods in hand, they started jumping behind walls or tried to disguise themselves as convection heaters. And still I kept—and keep on—baking.

I need to make something clear: baking may not be for you and if it isn't, I'm sorry and I hope you find something that helps. I also need to tell you that baking hasn't "cured" me. But it gets me through. My challenge—everyone's challenge—is about living through today and I find that baking passes the time. To be perfectly blunt about it, my choice sometimes is: I can kill myself or I can make a dozen cupcakes. Right so, I'll do the cupcakes and I can kill myself tomorrow.

Baking makes me concentrate on what's right in front of my nose. I have to focus. On weighing the sugar. On sieving the flour. I find it calming and rewarding because, in fairness, it is sort of magic—you start off with all this disparate stuff, like butter and eggs, and what you end up with is so totally different. And also delicious.

The thing is that I was absolutely clueless. I was a total beginner and I had to learn everything. I've taught myself to bake by doing it over and over again, and while I'm not claiming to be any sort of expert—I've made tons and tons of mistakes along with tons and tons of cakes—I've learned the basics and all kinds of handy little helpful tips and am delighted to share them with you.

Funnily enough, the part I enjoy most is the decorating. I say "funnily" because all my life I was famed in my family for being "bad with my hands." I was always terrible at drawing and sewing and I hated wrapping presents—I hadn't the patience to cut the paper neatly or tear off the right amount of tape. But it turns out that I can ice a cake. I've learned how to—would you believe!—use a piping bag and I've become a dab hand in nozzle work.

But don't be alarmed, no one is going to make you do nozzle work; this is a book about baking. I've included my favorite recipes. Some are very straightforward and simple because that was all I could handle at the time. And some are more complex—for example, the Banana Meringue Pie (see page 147) involves baking pastry, making a custard, and making the meringue—because there were times when I needed a challenge, when I needed to concentrate hard.

Either way, I can promise you that they're all delicious and I hope that you get some pleasure from making them. And indeed eating them.

Equipment List

I didn't own a single baking accoutrement the day the urge to bake came "at" me, literally not a thing. I had to get in my car and drive to the local supermarket (I had no idea that specialized cake equipment shops existed back then) and buy a couple of basic layer cake pans, along with the ingredients. Since then I've discovered that there's a whole universe of baking tools out there and I've acquired stuff on an as-needed basis. To be honest it feels like the more I get, the more I want, but I'm like that about everything. Once I start buying into a need, any need, it kick-starts some bottomless, insatiable black hole in me.

Don't get me started on cookie cutters. I'd been alive on the planet for several decades without ever knowing they even existed until one day I happened to be in a bakeshop and saw an adorable little metal thing in the shape of a handbag. I was charmed beyond belief, and purchased it with alacrity, warm with love and certain that it was the only cookie cutter I would ever need in my whole life. This state of satisfied bliss lasted approximately 7 seconds. Then I saw a cutter in the shape of a shoe and was filled with a terrible agony of want, so I got that one too. Briefly the beast was quieted. Then my appalling, needy eyes alighted on a quartet of stars, sized from dinky to large, and the longing started all over again. Since then I've gone on to acquire cookie cutters in the shape of cars, hearts, circles, flowers, fairy wings, stars, owls, moose, bats, beer mugs, football boots, rabid dogs, gangrenous legs, rotten teeth . . . and still I want more. If I had every cookie cutter in the world, it still wouldn't be enough.

Anyway, I digress. Here is a list of the most basic equipment you'll need:

Mixing bowl

Whatever kind you like. Those old-fashioned beige ceramic ones keep your ingredients cold, so they are good for doing pastry. Also, they have a certain stern retro air, a certain "I know what I'm doing" look to them, which can work well to intimidate guests to your kitchen. For myself, I have a blue plastic bowl.

Electric mixer

In the beginning, I managed fine with the cheapest possible handheld one, but after a certain mileage, the motor burned out on me. (In fairness, I was making cakes around the clock. I was like a wartime munitions factory and no machine could have withstood my frenzied demands.) Obviously, the more you pay, the more functions and stuff you get, all the way up to the gadget du jour, a KitchenAid. "An extra pair of hands," to quote their marketing. (No, I didn't get a free one from them. I haven't gotten free anything from anyone. If I recommend anything, it's only because I think it's good.)

Sieve

For getting the lumps out of flour or confectioners' sugar. Also—this came as a surprise to me—to add air to the mix, thus ensuring light and fluffy cakes.

Cake pans

Springform ones are lovely and handy for getting the cakes out without sticking. Also, silicone molds work great and are, of course, modern, space-age, and exciting. (Remember to put them on a baking sheet before you add the cake mixture because otherwise they'll flop all over the place and spill everything.) If you're wondering which width pan to start with, 8 inches is probably the most used size. Get two. Also, something that I find I use incessantly is an 8-inch-by-8-inch square pan.

Pie plate

If you're planning on making pastry, it would do no harm to get a pie plate—it can be metal or ceramic, and is very similar to a cake pan, except that the edges slope outward. A width of 8 inches or 9 inches should cover most eventualities. An extra complication is that pie plates come in different depths. I'd recommend that your first purchase be a "shallow" one, which is about 1¼ inches deep. And in the fullness of time you might get yourself a "deep" one, which has a depth of 2 inches.

Cupcake pan

To "hold" your paper liners because, left to its own devices, cake mix will push against the folds in the paper, will spread like wildfire and you'll end up with pancakes rather than cupcakes.

Purple silicone spatula

If you can't get purple, I suppose another color would do. This device is so brilliant at scraping your bowl, you'll probably get an extra half cake out of the mix. Sadly though, it means there's less left to lick. Or is that such a bad thing? One of the few downsides of being a keen baker is "getting high on your own supply." I'd somehow convinced myself, as I shoveled raw cake into my mouth, that if it wasn't cooked, it didn't count. I was wrong.

Palette knife

You may not need this as such, but if you're anything like me, you'll really enjoy it. I adore my palette knife. I love its beautiful strength and flexibility and sometimes I nip into the kitchen and spend a few happy minutes bending it backward and forward, cocking my ear for the faint but beautiful "whop-whop" noise it makes. It's almost a hobby in itself, like bursting bubble wrap.

Parchment paper

Important fact—wax paper is NOT the same as parchment paper. No. Wax paper is a ho-hum product that was used to line cake pans back in the olden days but often failed in its job and stuck to cakes, stuck to pans, and often made a hash of things. Parchment paper, on the other hand, is newfangled magical stuff and never sticks to anything.

Apron

Okay, maybe it's not vital, but it's a laugh.

Wire cooling rack

It lets hot air evaporate from your just-baked cakes, so that they don't end up continuing to cook in their own steam.

Digital weighing scale

Not as expensive as it sounds—don't let the word "digital" alarm you. But accuracy is important in baking. They say cooking is an art and baking is a science. Chemical reactions happen during baking and it's actually a very delicate business.

Airtight tin

All a bit Cath Kidston and retro, I know, but you want your stuff to stay fresh. The smaller stuff lasts the shortest amount of time. Make sure your baked goods are fully cooled before you put them into the airtight tin because the heat and the anaerobic atmosphere will mean germs will be having the time of their life in there, dancing, riding, and procreating at a ferocious rate, otherwise.

Basic icing kit

Icing is a whole universe in itself and to go into detail about it would fill at least a whole other book. But if you'd like to be able to have a little bit of fun and do basic swirls and stars and suchlike on top of cupcakes, why not treat yourself to a little beginners' kit. There are lots on the market, all containing a selection of differently shaped nozzles, some piping bags, and an instruction booklet. Wilton does a good one, but I'm sure most other brands are fine as well. Also, there is no shame at all in using pre-made writing icing—I use Betty Crocker decorating icing all the time.

Sugar paste gun

I'm joking. I mean you can if you want, but you'd want to be in a bad way, obsession-wise.

Some Rules

Only a few, but they'll help.

1. **Don't be afraid.** Really. It's only cake. Even if it's a disaster—and there will be times when despite your doing everything perfectly it will be—it's not the end of the world. While it's vital to follow recipes, we must remember we're still dealing with organic stuff—flour, butter, fruit and all that; one bag of sugar cannot be guaranteed to behave exactly the same as another. Also every oven is different. Even in the one oven, conditions can be different! (Once you start moving in baking circles you might hear talk of the famed "hot spot," a part of your oven that is inexplicably hotter than all the rest of it.) What I'm trying to say is that sometimes even when you do everything right, things will go wrong. Sometimes bad cakes happen to good people. It is not your fault.

2. **Before you begin making a cake, before you crack a single egg, read through the entire recipe**—ingredients, equipment required, and oven temperatures—from start to finish.

3. **For cakes and cupcakes have your eggs, butter, and milk at room temperature.** Take them out of the fridge about an hour before you start.

4. **For making pastry, on the other hand, have everything as *cold* as possible**—the ingredients, the bowl, and especially your hands. Some people are born with "hot hands"—genetics have dealt them a marked card. I am one of those misfortunates, and well-meaning, chilly-handed types have advised me to give up on pastry and stick to cake. But I've decided to defy the odds, to challenge the limitations I was born with. So yes, I make pastry. It won't be winning any prizes, but I like doing it.

5. **Have your pan lined or greased before you start,** especially if you're dealing with rising agents (e.g., baking soda, baking powder, or self-rising flour.) When your rising agent comes into contact with liquid (e.g., eggs or milk), a chemical reaction begins and gas is generated, but only for a short period of time. You don't want that gas ebbing away into the ether, instead you want that gas inside your cake, raising it and making it light and fluffy. So as soon as you add whatever rising agent you're using, you've got to get the whole business into cake pans and into the oven as quickly as possible.

6. **After you've put your cake in the oven, it is imperative that you don't open the door for as long as possible.** If you're new to baking you might be dying to see how it's all getting on in there. This is natural. A bit like the first time you applied fake tan, perhaps, and had to check every 5 minutes if it was coming up. And when nothing was happening, adding a bit more. Then more. Then ending up madly orange and streaky several hours later. Patience and restraint are what's called for. Resist the urge to open the oven door every 30 seconds. The cold air from outside will rush in and interfere with the rising process and you'll end up with a sunken, miserable cake. A "flop," quite literally.

7. **Also, if you were planning on having a temper tantrum and doing a lot of stomping and door-slamming in the kitchen region, now might not be the best time.** Cakes are sensitive little flowers and are easily distressed by loud noises. Could you hold off until your cake is done?

8. **Ingredients go funny after a while, even the dry goods; they sort of "die."** Baking powder loses its mojo, so does self-rising flour, and dried spices turn to a dust of nothingness. There are times when people end up with cakes that are flat and tasteless and they wonder what they've done wrong and maybe they've done nothing wrong, maybe it's just that their ingredients were past it. My suggestion is that if you bake only once a decade, why not treat yourself to a new bag of flour.

Techniques and Helpful Hints

Lining a loaf pan with parchment paper

When lining a pan, a technique you might find useful to get the parchment paper to stay where you want it to is to cut one piece big enough to cover the base and come right up the sides. Then—yes, I know it sounds strange—crumple it into a small ball and open it out again. Something about being crumpled makes it more pliable and less airy and floaty.

Salted or unsalted butter?

You get your unsalted fundamentalists. Many cake recipes are adamant that only unsalted butter will do, and round where I live, unsalted butter is like a shy woodland creature—an elusive, obscure thing. Sometimes it's in the shop and other times it isn't. You might get lucky, or then again you might not, but you can never bank on getting it. In my early days of baking, I thought that if I couldn't get the unsalted stuff that there was no point at all in using the salted stuff, but it turns out that I'm wrong—salted butter works fine for baking. In fact, I went on to discover that there are as many pro-salted butter advocates as there are unsalted. Experiment. These are your cakes. The choice is yours.

Melting chocolate

Now, about melting chocolate. What you need to know is that it must be done with great caution. A skittish, unpredictable beast is chocolate when it comes to being melted. Burns at the drop of a hat. Also, it does something called "seizing," which basically means it gathers together in a stubborn, surly ball and can't be coaxed to do anything else, just like a brokenhearted teenager. So you've two choices:

You can melt your chocolate by breaking it into a heatproof bowl and setting the bowl over a saucepan of simmering water. But don't let a single drop of water get on the chocolate, don't even let the bottom of the bowl sit in the water, else things will be seizing left, right, and center.

Or you can melt chocolate by breaking it into pieces and microwaving it, but listen to me: do it in 30-second bursts at half power and stir it between each bout, even when—and I can't stress this enough—*even when it looks exactly the same as the last time you saw it* 30 seconds previously.

One final note—white chocolate "suffers with its nerves." It's even more prone to burning than dark or milk chocolate, so take extra care with it.

Whatever melting method you use, do it slowly.

"Scalding" milk or cream

This means heating it until it's almost boiling, but without actually letting it boil. This involves standing over the stove, staring unblinkingly at the milk, every nerve and sinew strained. Don't feel foolish, this is the only way. When the perfect temperature is achieved, whip the pan off the heat.

Separating eggs

When you have to separate several eggs, a handy trick is to use 3 bowls. This way, if you accidentally spill yolk into your white, or (horrors!) get a bad egg, at least the damage is confined to just one egg and not the whole batch.

Begin by cracking your first egg. Let the white pour into what will henceforth be known as Bowl No. 1—basically this is an interim bowl, you're simply using it as a middleman. When as much of the white as you can extract is in Bowl No. 1, tip the yolk into Bowl No. 2 (also known at the **Bowl of Shame**, see page 144). Then! Empty the contents of Bowl No. 1 into your third bowl, now known as Bowl No. 3. Start on the next egg. Pour the white into Bowl No. 1, the yolk into the Bowl of Shame, then empty the contents of Bowl No. 1 into Bowl No. 3. And so on.

Banishing egg shell

If you accidentally get some egg shell in your egg white, what you must do is to scoop it out with another piece of egg shell. I know it sounds counterintuitive to be adding even more unwelcome shell, but this really works.

Baking blind

Not, as you might imagine, baking with a bandana around your eyes as if you're about to face a firing squad. No. This is a method of baking a pastry shell before the filling goes in. Once the raw pastry is in the pan, line it with a layer of parchment paper and weight it down with something. I use dried beans, but you can get gorgeous little glass balls from specialized baking shops. Blind baking achieves two things:

* The pastry under the filling will be cooked and therefore not soggy.

* The weight of the beans (or gorgeous little glass balls) will stop the pastry from rising and puffing and generally becoming unsuitable to "receive" filling.

Making a cookie base for cheesecake

To crush the cookies for the base, break them up roughly, put them in a plastic bag, and tie a knot in it. Then put that plastic bag in another plastic bag (you'll see why in a minute). Reach for a blunt instrument. I personally favor a mallet, but you can use a hammer, a rolling pin, even a wine bottle, basically anything that can inflict grievous bodily harm.

Belt and bash until the cookies turn to dust. You'll see now why you need the second plastic bag, because in all the excitement you might accidentally tear the first one and have crumbs all over the kitchen. (Can I just point out that you can save yourself all of this work if you have a food processor, but sometimes it's the journey itself that's enjoyable.)

Getting your cheesecake out of the pan

I've uncovered a conspiracy of silence around this and no recipe ever seems to address it. Here's what I've learned the hard way. Use a springform pan, but don't spring the catch until the very last moment. By then the lengthy period of refrigeration will have caused the cake to contract slightly and "pull" away from the sides of its container. Gently slide your palette knife between the pan and cake and methodically work it all the way round. When you feel the cake has been fully loosened from the pan, then—AND ONLY THEN—do you spring the catch. That part of the pan should lift off easily.

So that's the outside done. How do you get the base off? A lot trickier. Do you think the cake looks and feels firm enough to do the "two-plate" trick? If so, place a big flat plate facedownward on top of the cheesecake. It's important that the plate is flat. If it has an indent, no matter how shallow, it can cause the cake to crack and, Christ knows, no one wants that to happen. Slide one hand under the base of the cheesecake and place the other hand on top of the facedownward plate so that you're actually sandwiching the cake between your hands. However, now is not the time to start thinking about the terrible responsibility of that. Action is key. Keeping your fingers spread and your hands wide, working quickly, but smoothly, flip the cake over, so that now it's sitting upside down on the plate. The base of the pan will still be attached to it, but using your palette knife, gently, gently, gently ease it off, leaving your lovely cookie base behind.

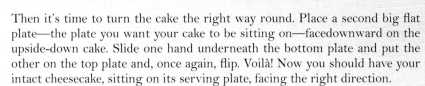

Then it's time to turn the cake the right way round. Place a second big flat plate—the plate you want your cake to be sitting on—facedownward on the upside-down cake. Slide one hand underneath the bottom plate and put the other on the top plate and, once again, flip. Voilà! Now you should have your intact cheesecake, sitting on its serving plate, facing the right direction.

Sometimes, when I've taken the springform edging off, I fear my cheesecake looks a little too wobbly and fragile to survive this traumatic two-plate process, and then I think, No, I'll be kind to it, I'll simply serve it on the base of the pan.

Glitter, sprinkles, sparkles, sugar balls, etc.

I get as much pleasure from decorating cakes—particularly cupcakes—as I do from baking them. To ice a cupcake and then to create a piece of edible art on top of it from glitter, sugar flowers, writing gel, fondant stars, etc. is the most wonderful feeling. An ordinary supermarket will have some sprinkles on their shelves, but to get some idea of the universe of decorations available to you, I'd really recommend that you go to a specialized bakeshop or website (www.cakeart.com is divine). You'll be dazzled and amazed and want to buy everything on it. You'll have the most wonderful time, I promise you.

How do you know when your cake is cooked?

Well, it tells you. If you press it gently and it "replies," i.e., springs back, you're in business. Or you can do the **Skewer Test**. Also known as the Toothpick Test. Basically, what happens is, when the allotted baking time is up, you stick a skewer (or indeed a toothpick) into the middle of the cake, then pull it straight back out again. If the skewer has cake mix sticking to it, you're not done yet. But if it comes out clean, the cake is cooked. Huzzah.

CLASSICS

It's not my way to keep things simple. No matter what I'm doing, I get a wild urge to up the ante. But in this section, I'm showing some respect. These recipes have been around for a long time and they've survived because they're so great. I remember lots of them from my childhood, and making any of these is a great way to start baking or to reintroduce yourself to baking if you've been away from it for a while.

Rock Cakes

Rock Cakes. Well, when I was growing up, they were considered a bit of a joke. The fault was definitely in the name—a cake that advertised itself as similar to a rock had to be hard and joyless, right? I made them countless times in Home Economics—oddly, they're the only things I actually can remember baking in that class—but I've no memory of what they tasted like. I don't think I even bothered to eat them. At the time I was obsessed with Yorkies and I had no interest in any kind of sweetmeat that wasn't shop bought.

However, I believe Rock Cakes have recently undergone a radical image makeover and are in big demand at children's birthday parties, thanks to Harry Potter being a fan of them. And now it transpires that the "Rock" of the title doesn't refer to the inedible hardness of the cakes, but the fact that they look like rocks. With this in mind, I recently remade them, and what a surprise! They're lovely. Sweet and crumbly and nothing like rocks! The key, according to my mother-in-law, Shirley, is to eat them pretty much as soon as they're baked.

Makes 14–16

1¾ cups self-rising flour
1 teaspoon baking powder
½ cup (1 stick) butter
1¾ cup golden raisins
1¾ ounces candied peel
⅓ cup superfine sugar
1 egg, beaten
about 3 tablespoons milk

To decorate

3 tablespoons turbinado sugar

Line a large baking sheet with parchment paper and preheat the oven to 400°F.

Sift the flour and baking powder into a large bowl, then rub in the butter until it resembles bread crumbs (or get your machine to do it). Stir in the raisins, candied peel, superfine sugar, and the beaten egg, mixing well together, until you have a stiff dough. If it's too stiff, add milk by the tablespoon, remembering you can always add more if you need it but it's a lot harder to take out if you've added too much.

Using 2 tablespoons—one for scooping, the other for scooping off (if you get me)—place golf ball–sized mounds of the mixture onto the prepared baking sheet, leaving space for spreading between each one. Do not worry yourself about making these boyos look smooth—remember they're meant to look craggy. The clue is in the name.

Sprinkle the top of each little mound with turbinado sugar, then bake for 15 to 20 minutes, until the cakes have gone golden brown. Cool on a wire rack and eat before too long. Gadzooks, or By Gor, or whatever it is that Harry Potter says.

Rhubarb Crumble

This is a pure delight to make because it's so quick and easy—you don't have to pre-cook the rhubarb, you just fling everything into the dish and it all cooks together, fruit and topping.

However, it kills me to keep things simple, it really does. I can't *bear* that this isn't Rhubarb, Lychee, and Star Fruit Crumble. Or Rhubarb, Kiwi, and Greengage Crumble. But I made a promise to you at the beginning of this section that I'd keep things classic and, really, I'm trying my best. Nevertheless, I've taken the small liberty of suggesting sprinkling a tiny teaspoon of dried ginger over the rhubarb because it brings out the flavor. And I've wondered if we might add some rolled oats into the crumble topping, because oats are so good for us and they make the topping extra crunchy. But if you are a crumble purist and I've offended you with my audacity, then, of course, omit the dried ginger, substitute ¾ cup all-purpose flour for the oats, and we will never refer to the matter again.

Serves 6–8

For the fruit base

2 pounds rhubarb

¼ cup turbinado sugar

1 teaspoon ground ginger

For the crumble topping

1½ cups all-purpose flour

¼ cup superfine sugar

¼ cup dark brown sugar

7 tablespoons butter, chilled and cut into cubes

1¼ cups rolled oats

Preheat the oven to 400°F.

Wash and trim the rhubarb stalks, slicing any that are particularly thick in half lengthwise first, then cut into chunks about 1 inch long and toss them in a bowl with the sugar and ginger, if you're using it. Empty the fruit layer ingredients into a 1½-quart pie plate (no need to grease) and press down.

For the topping, sift the flour into a bowl, then add the sugars and cold butter cubes (it is vitally important that the butter is cold because if it isn't we'll end up making more of a pastry than a crumble). If you're using a food processor, pulse on short bursts and keep a close eye on things. If you're rubbing in by hand, keep at it until the mix starts to look like a crumble. Add the oats, mix well, and sprinkle over the rhubarb mixture, making sure all the fruit is well covered.

Bake for 40 to 45 minutes or until the topping is golden brown. Serve warm, with custard or vanilla ice cream.

John's Sticky Toffee Pudding

So I said to Himself, "How do you make Sticky Toffee Pudding?" And he said, "I haven't a clue," and I said, "Well, that's very strange, seeing as it's your favorite dessert," and he said, "It's not my favorite dessert, I don't have a favorite dessert, I don't really like desserts at all," so I said, "Well, *who's* favorite dessert is it then?" And he said, "My dad's." Then he said, "You're always doing this, mixing me up with my dad." And I gave him a saucy look and said, "Well, *not always*."

Anyway! I consulted Himself's dad (whose name is John, a lovely, lovely man) and he gave me this wonderful recipe. It was fascinating to me because, although I've had Sticky Toffee Pudding many times, I'd never really focused on what's in it. Like, who knew about the dates? And the Horlicks? Although John says you can leave the Horlicks (or malted milk powder) out if you like. It gives a tiny hint of malt, but if that's not for you, just skip it. I have to say though, that this pudding (or cake, which is what this really is) is all about the toffee sauce. When you make the sauce you might think you've much too much. Believe me, you haven't.

Finally, just for a bit of fun, I've recommended an optional garnish. Do you know those really, really hard toffee-flavored sucky sweets? I think they're called Werther's Originals. The ones I found described themselves as "butter candies." Well, unwrap fourteen or fifteen of them and put them in a small plastic bag. Put that small plastic bag inside another small plastic bag, tie a knot in the bag, then take a big mallet and bash the living daylights out of the sweets until they're reduced to small shards of delicious toffee-flavored dust. Sprinkle over the pudding and sauce just before serving.

Serves 9

For the pudding

7 ounces Medjool dates
(the weight after the
pits have been removed)

1 teaspoon baking soda

4 tablespoons (½ stick) butter

¼ cup superfine sugar

2 eggs

1 heaping tablespoon Horlicks
(or malted milk powder)

1 teaspoon vanilla extract

1¼ cups self-rising flour

For the toffee sauce

¾ cup (1½ sticks) butter

1 scant cup light brown sugar

1 scant cup heavy cream

To decorate (optional)

14 or 15 butter candies, bashed
to smithereens

Butter an 8-inch square pan and preheat the oven to 350°F. Pit the dates if necessary, then chop them roughly. Put them in a bowl with the baking soda and cover with ¾ cup boiling water. Leave to stand for 10 minutes to soften, then drain away the water and whizz the dates in a food processor until they form a puree.

Meanwhile, cream the butter and sugar until pale. Add the eggs, Horlicks, and vanilla extract. Sift in the flour, then fold in the pureed dates. Pour the mixture into the prepared pan.

Bake for about 30 to 35 minutes. When the cake is done it will look—perhaps alarmingly—flat. Please don't fret. Remember what I said about this being all about the sauce. Put the pan on a wire rack.

While the cake/pudding is cooling, make the toffee sauce by putting the butter, sugar, and cream into a heavy-bottomed saucepan over a low heat until the sugar has dissolved and the butter has melted. Increase the heat a little and stir constantly. After a while, perhaps 10 minutes, the sauce will thicken and darken in color.

By now it should be possible to take the cake out of the pan without burning the hands off yourself. Cut into nine equal-sized squares and drown them in sauce. Sprinkle with crushed candies.

Simple Chocolate Mousse

This is gorgeous. Beautiful texture. Light, airy and—yes!—moussey.

7 ounces dark chocolate
  (70% cocoa solids)

4 eggs, separated

2 tablespoons superfine
  sugar

1 cup heavy cream

To decorate (optional)

squirty cream from a can

chocolate vermicelli
  sprinkles

Melt the chocolate using your preferred method (see page 20). Let it cool a little, then whisk in one of the egg yolks. When you feel it's fully absorbed, whisk in the next and so on until they're all in. There's a chance that the mixture might go a bit "congealy." If you feel it's too thick, add a tablespoon of water. Even two.

In a separate bowl, whisk the 4 egg whites until they start forming soft peaks. Add the sugar and keep whisking until stiff peaks form. In yet another bowl, beat the cream until soft peaks (yes, more peaks) form. Add a third of the chocolate/yolky mix to the cream and mix well. Add another third, beat well, then add the final third. Then, using a big metal spoon, fold the egg whites into the cream/chocolate mixture, trying to mix well while "keeping" the air (a next-to-impossible task if you ask me, but let's try our best).

Divide the mousse into four or six glasses. I'm just talking about ordinary drinking glasses. I used ones with 1½-cup capacity, but you can use smaller ones, or indeed bigger ones—imagine a pint of chocolate mousse, God, what a beautiful thought! Or, of course, you can use bowls. The good thing about using glasses is that you get to see the mousse before you eat it, which adds to the thrill, I think.

However! Yes, I'm afraid that there *is* a however—for every credit there is a debit—and the downside of using glasses is that the mousse spills down the sides of the glasses, both inside and outside, and the mess has to be cleared up. Amigos, I spent *hours*, and the best part of an entire roll of paper towels, carefully wiping the glasses so that they would be fit to present to my expected guests. (Actually, I had no expected guests. I live in an imaginary world and I planned to eat all four mousses myself.) I think I could have made things easier for myself if I'd used differently shaped glasses, ones that were wider at the brim than they were at the base. Like I keep saying, I make the mistakes so that you don't have to.

Chill for at least 3 hours. Decorate, if you like, with a squirt of cream from a can and a sprinkle of chocolate vermicelli sprinkles, but there's no need. It looks and tastes wonderful naked and unadorned.

Himself's Millionaire's Shortbread

Himself has no interest at all in sweet things. So all this cake stuff has been very boring for him. Nevertheless, he has been monumentally patient as I drone on beside him, chatting away to myself about superfine sugar versus turbinado sugar versus golden syrup. So there we were one day, me "bouncing ideas off him" (i.e., forcing him to sit and endure while basically I intoned, "Cake, cake, cake, cake, cake, cake, cake, cake," over and over again) and somehow the conversation strayed on to Millionaire's Shortbread and how hard it would be to make. To my great surprise, he suddenly became very animated and stopped looking like a man considering setting himself on fire, sat up straight, and said, "No, it's really easy! I used to make it when I was a teenager!"

I can't tell you! It was like discovering he was secretly Argentinian and had enjoyed a moderately successful career as a polo player in his twenties. Intrigued, I pressed him further for details and this is what he gave me.

Makes 16

For the base

1¾ cups all-purpose flour

5 tablespoons superfine sugar

¾ cup (1½ sticks) butter, cut into cubes

For the caramel layer

1½ cups sweetened condensed milk

14 tablespoons (1¾ sticks) butter

¼ cup golden syrup (or substitute dark corn syrup)

For the chocolate topping

5 ounces milk chocolate

5 ounces dark chocolate (70% cocoa solids)

Butter an 8-inch square pan and line the base with parchment paper. Make sure the pan is at least 2½ inches deep. Preheat the oven to 325°F.

Sift the flour into a bowl. Add the sugar and butter. If you have a machine, blitz everything together until you have a sandy-looking mixture, but beware of overmixing—you don't want this to turn into a dough. If you don't have a machine, I'm afraid you'll have to rub in the butter by hand. Pile the mixture into the prepared pan and prick the surface several times with a fork.

Bake for 30 to 40 minutes, until it's no longer pale-looking. Don't let it overbake and become hard and crusty because you'll have trouble down the line when you come to cut it. Leave to cool on a wire rack.

Now for the caramel layer. Put the condensed milk, butter, and golden syrup into a heavy-bottomed saucepan and heat gently. Then, whisking constantly, bring the temperature up until you reach bubbling point and keep it there for 5 to 8 minutes. Don't make the mistake that I did in the first few minutes of thinking that if the butter was melted, that we were bombs away. Himself came in, took one look at it, and said, "No, it's way too pale," so I had to put the saucepan back on the heat for at least another 10 minutes. Don't be tempted to turn up the heat any farther! The caramel must be made over a low heat to avoid it catching and burning. Eventually, the mixture will thicken and darken and change, so that when you allow the mixture to fall off the whisk, it makes light ribbons on the surface of the caramel.

Pour the caramel on top of the shortbread base and leave to cool for about an hour. For the chocolate topping, melt the chocolate (see page 20) and pour it over the caramel layer. Leave to set, but not in the fridge, for at least a couple of hours.

Remove from the pan and carefully cut into sixteen cubes.

Christmas Cake without Fear (aka Traditional Fruitcake)

The very words "Christmas Cake" bring memories of my childhood flooding back in an absolute avalanche. The Day the Christmas Cake Was Made was one of the biggest on the Keyes' calendar and *entre nous*—and perhaps unexpectedly—not always the most joyful.

It was usually done about a month before Christmas and my poor mother, the stress of it was terrible for her. The whole deal was TCMNF (The Cake Must Not Flop). And apparently anything—anything—could make the cake flop. Any loud noise. Any sudden movement. Any bad news. My memory is that we spent hours and hours and hours tiptoeing around the darkened house, conversing in whispers, the television and radio silenced. Under no circumstances must a shoe fall on the floor or a person burst into song (highly unlikely, given the tension). And if anyone opened the oven door, there was no telling, *simply no telling*, what awful consequences would ensue.

Another aspect that I vaguely remember—my stomach automatically clenching with cell-imprinted fear—was brown paper. The pan had to be wrapped in layer upon layer of brown paper, which extended far higher than the height of the pan. Like the silence, the brown paper was *of vital importance* to the success of the cake, and had to be secured with twine. (Love that word, twine. Far more interesting than mere string.) I could never get to the bottom of why the brown paper was needed—I've just rung my mother to ask her and she seemed to think it was something to do with preventing the cake from burning. (But she exhibited PTSD symptoms when I tried to get her to talk about it, so she's not the most reliable of witnesses. She told me that one year she was just so overwhelmed by the responsibility of Making the Christmas Cake that she gave up entirely and my brothers Niall and Tadhg came home from school to find her lying limp in an armchair, the cake half mixed and they—entirely clueless—had to take over. She says all she can remember from that terrible day is overhearing Tadhg saying, "Feck in another egg." Then a while later Niall saying, "Feck in more flour." She has no memory of how the cake eventually turned out because she says, "None of you ever ate it anyway. It was all about the selection boxes with you lot, I don't know why I bothered.")

Anyway! On that cheerful note, I've decided to reclaim Christmas Cake. This is very similar to my mother's recipe, but without the fear.

One very important thing to note is that you need to begin this cake an entire week before you actually bake it, because that's how long the dried fruit needs to steep in the brandy. (To be quite honest, if you're stuck for time, steeping it overnight should do fine.)　　　•••

Makes 14–16 slices

1½ cups currants

1¼ cups golden raisins

1¼ cups raisins

4½ ounces glacé cherries

2½ ounces chopped candied peel

1¼ cups brandy

1¼ cups (2½ sticks) butter, at room temperature

1½ cups light brown sugar

5 eggs

3 cups all-purpose flour

1 teaspoon allspice

1 teaspoon ground cinnamon

1 teaspoon ground ginger

½ teaspoon ground nutmeg

pinch of salt

⅔ cup ground almonds

grated zest of 1 lemon

Put the currants, golden raisins, raisins, cherries, and candied peel into a bowl and pour in the brandy. Cover the bowl with a cloth and leave to steep. Stir it daily so that, to quote my mother, "Everything gets a chance."

On the big day, begin by preparing your pan. Use an 8-inch square pan or a 9-inch round pan. Grease the base and sides of the pan with butter, then line the base and sides with two layers of parchment paper, making sure that it reaches at least 2½ inches above the edge of the pan. Preheat the oven to 300°F.

Cream the butter and sugar together until it's light, pale, and fluffy. In a separate bowl or pitcher, beat the eggs and add them slowly to the butter/sugar mixture, beating between each addition. If the mixture curdles, add a tablespoon of flour and keep going. Sift in the flour, spices, and salt and fold through by hand. Finally, fold in the soaked fruit, the ground almonds, and the lemon zest. My mother says, "You need a strong right arm for this." (Unless you're left-handed, of course.)

Transfer the mixture into the prepared pan, smooth the top out as best you can, then wrap the *outside* of the pan with yet another layer of parchment paper—tied in place with twine, of course. Or string, if you can't get any twine. Finally, as best you can, because this is undeniably a tricky business, loosely drape a layer of parchment paper over the top, so that the whole pan is encased in parchment paper. This is to stop the top of the cake from burning during the long baking process.

Bake for 4 hours, then do your Skewer Test (see page 23). The cake might not be done yet. Use your head and test regularly—perhaps every 15 minutes or so—until you're happy it's fully baked. Don't worry if it takes a long time. The cake just does take ages, it's a mammoth undertaking, it's as simple as that. Put the pan on a wire rack and wait until the cake is fully cooled before you begin the lengthy unwrapping process. Serve it as it is and it should be delicious and very densely fruity.

Okay, I know **CUPCAKES** have become a bit of a joke. I mean, we're overrun with the things. You can't go five yards without tripping over one. But they're ubiquitous for a reason: because they're lovely. They're an excellent little size. They're self-contained and unmessy in that you don't need a knife or a plate to eat them. And they can be decorated in the most adorable ways, which we'll get to.

For someone new to baking, cupcakes are brilliant because the ingredients are basic and the techniques are straightforward. The four basic requirements are flour, sugar, eggs, and some sort of fat, usually butter. Flavoring is up to you: it can be as simple as a teaspoon of vanilla extract, or you can experiment with chocolate, dried fruit, nuts, citrus rinds, even tiny pieces of licorice.

As for cupcake technique, have your butter and eggs at room temperature before you start. "Cream" the butter and sugar, that is, beat them together with gusto until "two-becomes-one" and they're fluffy and pale. What you're doing is incorporating air, which will help the end result be light and airy. Always beat your eggs before adding them to the mix and ALWAYS sift your flour. I've even heard of people "twice-sifting" their flour and sometimes even "three-times-sifting" (that is, sifting it onto a plate, then putting it back in the sieve, sifting it onto the plate again, then finally sifting it into the mixing bowl, all in an attempt to incorporate more air). Even for those of us looking for any small job to get us through the day, this seems a little excessive.

Once the flour has been sifted in, it's time for a change of pace. No more gusto-stirring. Gently, now, all is gentle. What's happening is that we're "folding" in the flour, that is, we're turning it into the mixture with as little energy as possible. This is still all about the "air"—we don't want to knock out the air we've gone to a lot of time and trouble to incorporate. Sometimes people suggest using a metal spoon for this exercise, but I prefer my purple spatula because it gets into all the nooks and crannies.

Using two tablespoons—one to scoop and the other to scrape off the scoopy one—dollop the mixture (or "batter" as some cake writers like to call it) into cupcake liners. The general rule is to fill the liner two-thirds full to leave space for the much-heralded "rising," but in some of the recipes here I've gone off piste with other suggestions.

Now, a word about cupcake liners. There is no standard size. When someone finally articulated this simple truth to me, it was as if I'd been let into the secret of the universe. I'd instinctively known that there was something I wasn't understanding when I was spooning cake mix into paper liners, but I didn't know what I didn't know, if you know what I mean. I now discover that there are different widths at the base, there are different widths at the top, there are different depths to the "pleats" and there are different heights. All different. God knows how many variables we've got on our hands and there is no right or wrong, but it's important to know what you're dealing with. Personally I favor the taller, narrower paper liner, but to each their own.

Bake at the suggested temperature for the suggested amount of time, but if you're not sure they're done, apply the Skewer Test (see page 23). Cool the pan on a wire rack for about 10 minutes, then—gently, because they're still very wobbly, like any newborn—take each cupcake, still in its paper liner, out of the pan, but keep them cooling on the rack for about half an hour. You can now serve them as they are, or you can decorate with an icing (see page 51 for the basic Glacé and Buttercream icings), the choice is yours.

B-List Chocolate-Chip Cupcakes

The more fat a recipe has, the richer and more delicious it is. Because this recipe has only one egg, a smallish amount of butter, and uses cocoa powder instead of melted chocolate, it's not the richest thing you'll ever taste, but you know what, it'll do grand. Like, it won't be disgusting or anything. It's quick and easy and good for serving to kids because they don't care about subtleties. Especially if you throw a few glittery sprinkles over the finished product. Or else you can balance the whole thing out by using a super-rich chocolate topping.

Makes 12

¾ cup self-rising flour

5 tablespoons cocoa powder (70% cocoa solids)

½ cup superfine sugar

3½ tablespoons butter

½ cup whole milk*

1 egg

½ teaspoon vanilla extract

½ cup milk chocolate chips (optional)

For the (optional) topping

3½ ounces dark chocolate (70% cocoa solids)

4 tablespoons (½ stick) butter, cut into cubes

2 cups confectioners' sugar

¼ cup whole milk

½ teaspoon vanilla extract

*Must be whole milk. Must be!

Preheat your oven to 325°F and line a 12-hole cupcake pan with paper liners.

Mix the flour, cocoa powder, sugar, and butter until the butter is absorbed and the whole business starts to look grainy. You can do this by hand, using an electric mixer, or, if you're lucky enough to have a KitchenAid, using the paddle attachment.

In a separate bowl, whisk the milk, egg, and vanilla extract together, then add to the flour mixture, taking care not to overmix. Throw in the chocolate chips, if you're using them, and distribute evenly.

Divide the mixture among the paper liners and bake for about 20 minutes, until the cupcake "replies" when pressed. Or use your Skewer Test (see page 23). Cool on a rack.

Make the (optional) topping by melting the chocolate and butter in a saucepan over a very low heat, stirring constantly, until they've melted. Remove from the heat and gradually beat in the confectioners' sugar, milk, and vanilla, whisking until smooth. If you feel the icing is looking too runny to use straight away, refrigerate for 15 to 20 minutes.

A word of warning. Because of the low fat content, these cupcakes won't last long, even in an airtight tin.

Consistently Reliable Cupcakes

Very dependable little creatures, these. They always come out just right—just moist enough, just light enough, just rich enough. I've used vanilla here, but there's a huge choice of flavoring available and there are a few variations suggested at the end. I've recommended icing these cupcakes with buttercream and again suggested flavoring with vanilla, but once more, feel free to use whatever flavoring you like.

Makes 12

9 tablespoons butter, at room temperature

½ cup superfine sugar

2 eggs, beaten

1 vanilla pod*

1 cup self-rising flour

Buttercream icing

1 cup (2 sticks) butter, at room temperature

2½ cups confectioners' sugar

1 teaspoon vanilla extract

gel or liquid food coloring (optional)

glitter or colored sanding sugar (again optional, but why not go for it?)

*Or if that's a bit too exotic and scary, a teaspoon of vanilla extract. But preferably not imitation vanilla, which is just a load of chemicals. Unless you're really stuck, and then work away. God knows, what harm can it do? I mean, they used to give babies gripe water, which is basically alcohol, and the human race has survived thus far.

Preheat your oven to 325°F if you'd like flat-topped cakes or 350°F if you'd like them round. Line a 12-hole cupcake pan with paper liners. IMPORTANT: ensure that you pick nice colors and patterns, ones that will make you happy.

Fling your butter into your bowl and cream the daylights out of it with an electric mixer, occasionally scraping the beaters with your purple spatula (see page 16). When you start to feel a little bored—perhaps after 5 minutes or so—add the sugar and keep beating until the whole mixture goes pale and fluffy.

Gradually add the eggs, beating well between each addition. Now brace yourself: the mixture might curdle a bit, but DON'T PANIC. You've done nothing wrong, this is not your fault. It is an occasional and unpleasant fact of life, like for example a burst tire, it happens to the best of us. Simply sift in a little of the flour, keep beating valiantly, and soon the problem will go away. If only everything in life was as fixable.

Next, the vanilla pod, not as daunting as it may sound. Slit it along its length and you will discover a load of seeds inside. Use a knife to scrape these out and fling them into the mixture. Discard the rest.

Abandon the beaters, sift in the flour, and then gently "fold" (i.e., incorporate) it into the mixture, using as few turns of the spatula (or metal spoon) as possible. When you can't see any more flour lurking in the bowl, you're ready to go. Using two tablespoons, distribute the mixture into the cupcake liners, filling them approximately two-thirds full.

Bake at 325°F for 22 minutes if you want flat-tops or 350°F for 18 to 20 minutes if you'd prefer dome-shaped. Or do the Skewer Test (see page 23). Cool on a wire rack and store in an airtight tin. They should keep for a day or so. Slightly longer if your tin has polka dots.

To make the icing, cut the butter into chunks into a bowl and slowly sift in the confectioners' sugar. On a very slow speed, beat the two together. When the confectioners' sugar is incorporated, you can increase the speed until the icing is smooth and creamy. Add the vanilla extract and food coloring, if you're using, and beat again.

Use a mini palette knife to smooth the icing over the tops of the cupcakes. Or if you're feeling brave, use a piping bag with a star-shaped nozzle and pipe fat swirls. Finish with a sprinkle of glitter, colored sanding sugar, or whatever you're in the mood for.

Variations

By omitting the vanilla pod, you can use this same basic recipe to make a variety of flavors. For example, if you'd like orange flavoring, add the zest of half an orange. Or add a teaspoon of coffee powder dissolved in 2 tablespoons of boiling water for coffee flavor (cool it slightly before adding because it might scramble the eggs). Or sift a teaspoon of ground ginger in with the flour for ginger flavoring, and so on.

Slightly Sinister Star Anise Cupcakes

Star anise is some sort of spice, with a sweet licorice, aniseedy flavor, which can be found in Asian food shops. I've also suggested adding actual pieces of licorice (the soft, good-quality stuff you get in health food stores) to this recipe, but if it's too full-on, reduce the amount or just leave it out altogether. Some people (particularly jazz lovers, I've found) are mad for these cupcakes, claiming that they're their absolute favorites, but others are a bit freaked out. Especially children. Sometimes they cry.

Just a quick note on fondant, in case you don't know what it is. It's a thick brick of icing that needs to be kneaded and softened, then rolled out. (You'll probably be most familiar with it from Christmas cakes.) Regular supermarkets sell it in white lumps, which you can color into a multitude of gorgeous hues using gel from specialist bakeshops. To make black fondant, mix it with black gel food coloring. Please don't be intimidated by fondant, it looks so fantastic on top of cakes.

Makes 12

4 star anise

¾ cup whole milk

½ cup (1 stick) butter

½ cup superfine sugar

2 eggs

½ teaspoon vanilla extract

1⅓ cups self-rising flour

½ teaspoon baking powder

pinch of salt

3½ ounces soft black licorice, original flavor, chopped very, very, very finely

For the icing

5 ounces black fondant

edible glue OR clear alcohol OR apricot jam that has been boiled and strained (to stick the sugar paste to the cupcakes)

5–6 pieces of soft black licorice, chopped very finely

Bash the star anise with a mallet, hammer, or any blunt instrument you might have handy. Pour the milk into a saucepan, then add the bashed star anise. "Scald" the milk (see page 21), then leave for at least an hour for the licorice flavor from the star anise to infuse into the milk.

When the hour is up, preheat the oven to 350°F and line a 12-hole cupcake pan with paper liners, preferably in a dark color (black would be ideal).

Cream the butter and sugar, then add the eggs and vanilla extract. Sift in the flour, baking powder, and salt. Using a sieve, strain the milk into the mixture, leaving the star anise behind. You can now discard these. Fold the mixture carefully until all the flour is incorporated, then add the small pieces of chopped licorice, distributing evenly.

Divide the mixture among the cupcake liners, bake for approximately 20 minutes, then cool on a wire rack.

You can serve them undecorated, but if you'd like to decorate them, lightly dust your surface with confectioners' sugar and roll out the fondant. Using one of your shamefully large collection of cookie cutters (if you're me), cut out twelve circles, each slightly wider than the surface of the cupcakes. Stick the circles of fondant onto the cupcakes using edible glue, clear alcohol, or apricot jam. Attach the pieces of licorice to the top of the cupcakes (see a photo of the cakes on page 61). Eat, wearing a black polo neck jumper and listening to mid-period Miles Davis.

Zeny's Banoffee Cupcakes

These aren't mere cupcakes, these are *events:* banana sponge with a heart of dulce de leche and luscious toffee-flavored cream cheese frosting.

I'd bought a big bunch of bananas in the vague hope that the potassium might help, but then I hadn't the energy to peel them. They were sitting on the countertop, getting more and more ripe while I was feeling more and more guilty, and then my lovely friend Beth was over and, without prompting, wrote out her sister Zeny's foolproof banana bread recipe, and suddenly I was reinvigorated.

I've adapted the recipe slightly to make it more suitable for cupcakes and I've added toffee to make the "offee" bit, but obviously you can leave it out and still have monumentally delicious banana cupcakes.

First, a word about dulce de leche. It's an Argentinian dessert, which literally translates as "sweet milk." (Mind you, the one time I was in Argentina I actually had it for my breakfast, but that's the type I am.) It's a delicious, gooey, toffee-caramel style thing with a texture like thick set custard. You could make it yourself, but it's a fiendishly tedious exercise because it involves hanging around a saucepan of simmering milk for the best part of a day. Also, I believe it can be produced by boiling a can of condensed milk for 4 hours (I saw it done by Emile Heskey's girlfriend on *Celebrity Come Dine with Me*), but then I read a horror story on the Internet about someone's saucepan boiling dry and the can of condensed milk exploding. So I buy my dulce de leche ready-made. Obviously, there's a variety of authenticity and quality available—there's some very high-class stuff, which is handmade by tango-dancing gauchos wearing shoes that used to belong to Eva Perón's next-door neighbor. Or you can buy it mass-produced in a can, which makes me feel a bit Jeremy Kyle, but it's actually delicious.

•••

Makes 12

½ cup (1 stick) butter

½ cup superfine sugar

2 eggs, beaten

3 or 4 very ripe bananas

1 cup self-rising flour

approx. 15 ounces dulce de leche (You'll only need about 3 ounces for the cakes, but you can use the rest for icing.)

For the icing

3½ tablespoons butter, at room temperature

3 ounces cream cheese, at room temperature

1½ cups confectioners' sugar

Preheat the oven to 325°F and line a 12-hole cupcake pan with paper liners.

Cream the butter and sugar until pale and fluffy, then add the beaten eggs. Mash the bananas and gently add to the mixture, then sift in the flour and fold until it's all absorbed.

Now, this is where the challenge begins. Using two tablespoons, and at times maybe even your fingers, distribute about two-thirds of the cake mixture into the paper liners, making sure the entire base of each liner is covered. Then—and this is the fiddliest bit—gently place a small round dollop, about the size of a malt ball, of dulce de leche into the middle of each cupcake. (I use a melon baller to do this, it gives a very handy shape and size.)

Next—again using your fingers if you have to, this is delicate work—distribute the remaining cake mixture into the paper liners, completely covering the dulce de leche and making sure that the edges of the "bottom" layer of cake mix are adhering to the top. The idea is that you're making a little dulce de leche bomb. On the outside it looks just like an ordinary cupcake. But then a person bites into it and—oho! A delightful caramelly surprise is awaiting within.

I'll be honest, getting these right can be tricky because you don't want the dulce de leche sinking to the bottom and just sort of leaking away. It's about having the base layer thick enough to withstand the weight, while still having enough cake mixture left over to put a lid on things and seal the whole little envelope.

Practice is the key. Practice and patience. Practice, patience, and perseverance. Practice, patience, perseverance, and persistence. (Can I think of anything else beginning with P? "Praise," how about that? Praise the cakes for holding up the dulce de leche. It's all about positive affirmation. If you tell them they can support the dulce de leche, then they'll believe they can.)

Bake for at least 25 minutes, maybe even half an hour. I know it sounds like a long time, but it's because of the bananas.

Now, for the icing. You can keep things simple and simply put a layer of dulce de leche on the top of each little cake. Or you can make things slightly more complicated by diluting the dulce de leche with cream cheese frosting.

Mix 14 ounces of the dulce de leche with the butter, cream cheese, and confectioners' sugar until it's thick and creamy, then smooth it over the cupcakes. Or, if you're feeling like more of a challenge, pile it all into a piping bag with a star-shaped nozzle and squeeze it out in big, fat, fabulous swirls.

Chocolate Cheesecake Cupcakes

Try saying that with loose dentures. These are very special—they're not really cupcakes at all, they're mini cheesecakes, but in cupcake format (albeit without the cookie base)—and they are *delicious*.

Makes 12

3½ ounces dark chocolate (70% cocoa solids)

9 ounces mascarpone cheese

7 ounces Philadelphia regular cream cheese*

½ cup superfine sugar

2 eggs

1 teaspoon vanilla extract

½ cup milk chocolate chips

*Not the low-fat version. Or the one with garlic and herbs.

Line a 12-hole cupcake pan with paper liners and preheat the oven to 300°F.

Melt the chocolate using your preferred method (see page 20). Beat the cheeses, then add the sugar, eggs, and vanilla extract and beat again. Using your purple spatula (see page 16), add the melted chocolate and mix well, then throw in your chocolate chips, doing your best to distribute them evenly, but not going all OCD about it.

Divide the mix among the paper liners. Fill generously. You might have a moment of panic when you think you have too much mixture, but the thing is that these cupcakes don't really rise, so it's okay to fill the liners almost to the top.

Now we're going to do something that sounds trickier than it actually is: we're going to "bain-marie" these boyos. Basically, you put your metal cupcake pan into a bigger, deeper pan (like a roasting pan, for example). Pour warm—not boiling—water into the bigger, deeper pan so that it comes about three-quarters of the way up the side of the cupcake pan, then place—with great caution—in the oven.

Bake for 40 minutes then—again, with great caution, in fact with much *greater* caution because by now the water is scalding hot—take it all out. Pour away the water and place the cupcake pan on a cooling rack. Leave it about an hour before you take the cupcakes out of the pan because they have to sort of "set." But you can't eat them just yet, they need to be refrigerated. Could you bear to do it overnight?

Serve with a dollop of whipped cream and, can I just say something, these cupcakes may not look like anything special, but when a person takes a bite, they sort of freeze, then they yelp, "Oh my good Christ, what just happened there?" And the next thing they're tearing at the cupcake with their nails, shoveling it into their mouths and lunging at you and demanding more.

Red Velvet Cupcake Swirls

According to my research, Red Velvets date from the olden days when cocoa powder was a much lighter color than it is now. During the baking process, the acid in the cake mix (sometimes provided by buttermilk, sometimes, as in this recipe, by vinegar) chemically reacted to create the distinctive red color. Nowadays though, with cocoa powder being so dark, the red color is provided by food coloring. Nevertheless, the yumminess remains the same.

It seems to be a given that Red Velvets are served with cream cheese frosting, but I've gone a little experimental here and incorporated a cream cheese layer into the mix, so the frosting is "built in," if you get me. It is "swirled through" and actually baked into each little cake, which not only looks beautiful but also means you don't have to do any decorating or icing at the end.

Makes 12

For the red velvet layer

7 tablespoons butter

¾ cup superfine sugar

1 teaspoon vanilla extract

½ cup cocoa powder

a pinch of salt

1 tablespoon red food coloring

1 teaspoon white wine vinegar

2 eggs

1¼ cups self-rising flour

For the cream cheese layer

7 ounces cream cheese, at room temperature

1 egg

¼ cup superfine sugar

½ teaspoon vanilla extract

Line a 12-hole cupcake pan with paper liners and preheat the oven to 325°F.

First, make the cream cheese layer by beating the cream cheese with the egg, sugar, and vanilla extract. Keep it standing by.

Make the red velvet mixture by melting the butter. Put into a bowl with the sugar and beat well. Next—in this exact order! Something to do with chemical jiggery-pokery that I can't explain, but must be observed—add the vanilla extract, the cocoa powder, the salt, the food coloring, and the vinegar, beating between each addition.

In a separate bowl, beat your eggs, then add to the butter/cocoa mixture. Sift in the flour and fold through.

Divide most of the mixture among the paper liners, reserving perhaps a fifth. Then, dollop a lump of cream cheese mixture into each paper liner on top of the red velvet mixture. *Then*, divide the remaining red velvet mixture into the paper liners, on top of the cream cheese mixture.

Now, *swirl*. You can use a toothpick, but I used a bamboo skewer—something with a bit of length is nice because you can get right down into the red velvet mixture and dredge up its murky depths—and twirl and swirl until the red and white mixtures are beautifully striped. This is an *extremely* enjoyable exercise, so enjoyable that I never want to stop, but I must because if I don't, the two mixtures will become one and the whole thing will be pointless.

Bake for 17 to 20 minutes. Cool fully on a wire rack.

Wasabi and White Chocolate Cupcakes with Salted Caramel Icing

Yes, I'm serious. Wasabi. The stuff you have with sushi. But trust me, this isn't a game of novelty cupcakes, this recipe is *gorgeous*. The sweetness of the white chocolate combined with the richness of the eggs is powerful enough to go head-to-head with the heat of the wasabi. Then, paired with the salted caramel icing, the whole experience becomes transcendent.

If you really remain unconvinced by the wasabi, just leave it out. It's a great cupcake recipe anyway—it gives a very moist, rich crumb. And the salted caramel icing is *amazing*. Make sure you use it in lots of recipes—on brownies, as a topping for ice cream, whatever you can think of.

Makes 12

For the cupcakes

3½ ounces white chocolate

7 tablespoons butter, chilled and cut into cubes

½ cup superfine sugar

1 teaspoon vanilla extract

3 eggs

½ cup all-purpose flour

1 teaspoon baking powder

pinch of salt

1 tablespoon wasabi paste

For the salted caramel topping

7 tablespoons butter

⅓ cup light brown sugar

¼ cup golden syrup (or substitute dark corn syrup)

1 teaspoon vanilla extract

1 teaspoon coarse sea salt

Line a 12-hole cupcake pan with paper liners and preheat the oven to 350°F.

Melt the chocolate using your favored method (see page 20), remembering that this is white chocolate and is easy to burn. Add the butter to the chocolate and stir until everything is melted and combined. Remove from the heat and stir in the sugar. The mixture might look a little strange and "congealy." Don't worry. Let it all cool for about 10 minutes, then add the vanilla extract and beat with an electric mixer for a full 3 minutes. This should sort out any nonsense. Add an egg and beat for at least 30 seconds. Add the next egg, and so on, until all are in. Sift in the flour, baking powder, and salt and fold through. Finally—if you're going to be brave—add the wasabi paste and make sure it's distributed evenly. Divide the mixture among the cupcake liners. Bake for 22 minutes. Cool the tray on a wire rack.

Meanwhile, make the salted caramel topping by putting the butter, brown sugar, golden syrup, vanilla, and salt into a heavy-bottomed saucepan and melt over a gentle heat. When the butter and sugar have melted, raise the heat. Whisk like mad until the mixture starts bubbling, but don't let it boil. Keep it at that bubbling point for about 5 to 8 minutes and it should thicken a little. But beware! This thing is horrifyingly hot and impossible to get off if you get splashed with it. Treat it with caution.

When you're satisfied with its consistency, let it cool a little before icing the cupcakes—if it's too hot, it's liable to run down the sides. However, if it cools down too much, it won't spread easily enough. So feel free to reheat it a bit if it's gotten too stubborn and resistant, or let it cool down if it's gone a little free-spirited with itself. Finish by sprinkling the top with a few grains of sea salt.

CHEESECAKES

"Black Hole" Chocolate Cheesecake

Individual Amaretto Cheesecakes

Blokey Snickers Cheesecake Loaf

Lavender and White Chocolate Cheesecake

No-Bake Ginger and Lime Cheesecake

Rosewater and Coconut Cheesecake

Fridge-Set Honeycomb Cheesecake

Upside-Down Saffron, Mint, and Pomegranate Cheesecake

There are two kinds of cheesecakes—the baked kind and the non-baked kind—and they're both GORGEOUS. **CHEESECAKES** are very much about the texture: the baked ones should be dense enough to get me to emit an involuntary low moan of pleasure and the non-baked should be smooth and creamy, but, either way, cheesecake is not the sort of thing to make if you're looking for INSTANT GRATIFICATION. If a sugar craving comes at you, find some other way of addressing it because the unvarnished truth is that some relationships last longer than the time it takes to make cheesecake.

It's not that there's huge amounts of work involved in baking cheesecakes, but there are long periods of waiting while some sort of magic happens, and I know of no way of speeding these up. But the wait is worth it, I promise you.

First, the base. Almost all of the recipes here involve melted butter mixed with some sort of crushed cookie—I've varied the cookies quite a bit because I started to become a little weary of graham crackers after a while. In some cases, I've recommended that the base be baked briefly, but all of them need to be refrigerated and ideally it should be overnight (or if you're really desperate, stick it in the freezer for 20 minutes).

The reason for this is to "set" the base to allow it to retain its own identity, if you know what I mean, so that the cheesecake itself doesn't just overrun and swamp it. Firm delineation between the two is important; your mouth needs to know what's going on. "Yes, I see," it should be able to think, "I'm currently eating the baked cheesecake part and I'm going to emit an involuntary low moan of pleasure, and now I'm eating something different. I'm eating the crunchy cookie base and my, how agreeable the contrast between the two textures is."

No-bake cheesecake usually sets in 3 hours, which might sound long, but it's nothing in comparison with the baked version, which is a right marathon. But as I keep saying, it's worth it. There is something about baked cheesecake that benefits from the aging process, like fine wine and George Clooney.

The mixing of the cheesecake itself is a simple enough business—all involving some combination of cream cheese, eggs, sugar, cream, and flavoring. And even the baking times aren't that long, between 40 minutes and an hour and a half. But when the baking time is up, I recommend that, without opening the oven door, you turn the heat off and let the cake stay in there, for at least an hour and possibly even overnight.

And even then it isn't ready to be eaten—it needs to be refrigerated. I'm so sorry! Could you bear to do it for 6 hours? Or even longer? I'm not just being cruel, something beyond our ken is happening inside the cheesecake. Strange forces are at work and at a molecular level it's changing and deliciousness is developing at an exponential rate.

Finally—and it might be 48 hours after you first started making it— your cheesecake will be ready to eat and I promise you, oh I promise you, you'll be glad you waited.

A couple of other points. In some recipes I call for using Philadelphia cream cheese, but you must use the full-fat version. You see, any so-called low-fat cheese has been diluted with air and water and you might be able to fool yourself that it's delicious on your slice of toast, but it'll ruin your cake. Also, try not to do what I did one unhappy evening and accidentally buy the Garlic and Herbs version.

Finally, see the Techniques and Helpful Hints section (page 22) for how to get your cheesecake out of the pan.

"Black Hole" Chocolate Cheesecake

So called because it's so dense it seems to collapse under the weight of its own fabulousness. Eating a slice of this is like being punched in the stomach with a chocolate-flavored fist. Stupendous.

Serves 10

For the base

3½ ounces dark chocolate (70% cocoa solids)

3½ tablespoons butter

7 ounces graham crackers

For the filling

7 ounces dark chocolate (70% cocoa solids)

7 ounces mascarpone cheese

7 ounces Philadelphia cream cheese—the full-fat variety*

¼ cup superfine sugar

2 eggs

1 teaspoon vanilla extract

¼ teaspoon black pepper**

½ cup heavy cream

*Remember what I said, you're only ruining it for yourself otherwise.

**I know, strange, but trust me.

Grease the sides and line the base of a 9-inch springform pan with parchment paper.

To make the base, melt the chocolate using your favored method (see page 20), then melt the butter in a saucepan.

Break the graham crackers roughly, using the method on page 22.

When the graham crackers are completely annihilated, mix them with the melted butter and chocolate, then press them into the springform pan, completely coating the base and bringing a little "lip" up the sides. To make the surface smooth and even, I've found—oddly—that pressing a potato masher against it does the job. Stick in the fridge for at least an hour.

To make the filling, preheat the oven to 325°F. Melt the chocolate and let it cool a little.

With much gusto, whip the cheeses with the sugar, eggs, vanilla, and black pepper. Really give this your best shot so all the lumps are gone. This is one situation where an electric mixer is a godsend. The first cake I ever made was this one—I did it all by hand and my arm nearly had to be hospitalized.

Pour in the cream and keep whisking. Finally add the cooling chocolate and—yes—keep whisking. When it's all mixed and there are no white bits left to be seen, pour the mix in on top of the set graham cracker base and bake for 40 minutes. Then, without opening the door, turn off the oven and let the cake sit in there for at least 2 hours, or preferably overnight.

During the cooking time, your cake will have risen, but it will slowly sink back into itself. This isn't a bad thing. Not at all. It is simply becoming the cheesecake version of a black hole, the densest, most chocolatey thing in the universe. When you finally remove it from the oven, you'll stagger under the weight.

But it's not time to eat it yet. No, I'm sorry! Into the fridge with it, for at least 6 hours, preferably overnight. It's harsh to deprive you, but this cake really benefits from the wait.

Finally, spring the catch on the pan and release the cake into the wild.

Individual Amaretto Cheesecakes

This recipe gives you 6 mini-cheesecakes, each one more than enough for one person. These are elegant, grown-up cheesecakes—the base comes courtesy of crushed amaretti cookies and the flavor of the filling is provided by amaretto liqueur. (The alcohol does evaporate during the cooking process, but if you'd prefer to steer clear, just use a teaspoon of almond extract instead.)

Makes 6

For the base

5 ounces amaretti cookies

3 tablespoons butter

For the filling

12 ounces Philadelphia cream cheese, at room temperature

⅓ cup superfine sugar

2 small eggs, separated

3 tablespoons amaretto liqueur

Preheat the oven to 300°F.

I suggest making these in a 6-hole muffin pan (the holes being 3 inches in diameter). Grease liberally. I'm lucky enough to own a silicone muffin "pan," so I don't have to grease anything, which I'm grateful for because even though it doesn't take long, I find it a tedious business. If you can't face the greasing process and you don't have a silicone pan, you could even use muffin liners.

Melt the butter and crush the amaretti cookies (see page 22 for cookie crushing suggestions). Mix the two together, then press down hard into the pan, using the base of a glass.

Bake for 15 minutes, take out of the oven, cool down, then refrigerate for at least an hour.

To make the filling, preheat the oven again to 300°F.

In one bowl, beat the cheese, sugar, and egg yolks. Add the amaretto or almond extract, whichever you're using.

In a separate bowl, beat the egg whites until soft peaks form. Gently fold this into the cheese mixture.

Still being gentle—you want to keep as much air as possible in this— spoon it on top of the amaretti cookie base.

Bake for 40 minutes. If you happen to glance through the oven window, you'll see that they'll puff up and rise alarmingly high, but don't worry, they'll calm down again.

When the 40 minutes is up, don't open the door, but turn off the oven, and leave the cakes sitting there for a couple of hours.

Then—yes, you've heard this before—refrigerate overnight.

Blokey Snickers Cheesecake Loaf

Snickers is an essentially blokey thing, no? I've always thought it's the sort of sweetmeat that men take a big chomp out of just before they rappel down the side of a mountain and, for a while, I thought it was the law that Snickers could only be eaten by men speeding past me on mountain bikes. Inspired by such rugged outdoorsiness, this is a hefty, hearty cheesecake, specially for the boys. The loaf format is an extra little touch on my part; I think it makes it even more manly.

Makes 10 substantial slices

For the base

5 ounces milk chocolate digestive cookies (or graham crackers if you can't find them)

⅓ cup salted peanuts

5 tablespoons butter

For the filling

9 ounces mascarpone cheese

9 ounces ricotta cheese

½ cup superfine sugar

2 eggs

¾ cup sour cream

4 Snickers bars, chopped into chunks

To decorate

squeezy toffee sauce out of a squeezy bottle

a generous handful of salted peanuts

Preheat the oven to 325°F.

Line a 2-pound loaf pan with parchment paper—see the technique on page 20.

In a food processor, whizz the digestive cookies and peanuts so they form a rough-cut, rustic-looking mixture; you should still be able to see parts of the peanuts. The first time I did it, I left the machine running so long that I accidentally made peanut butter and the whole thing went into a brown paste. Although I soldiered on, the base never really set, and I ended up having to do it all again. But that's okay, I make the mistakes so you don't have to.

Melt the butter and stir it through the crumbs. Even when you think it's fully mixed, give it a few more stirs. Pour the digestive cookie/peanut/butter mixture into the bottom of the loaf pan and pack down hard, using the base of a glass. Bake for 15 minutes, remove from the oven and cool, then refrigerate, preferably overnight.

To make the filling, preheat the oven again to 325°F. Mix the two cheeses together, then add the sugar and eggs. Pour in the sour cream, then stir in the Snickers pieces. Pour in on top of the cookie base.

Bake for an hour and a half, then turn off the oven and leave it sitting in there for as long as you can bear. When you eventually take it out, you'll be delighted to see the top has developed a gorgeous fudgey look. Refrigerate overnight.

To get the cake out of the pan, you'll need your palette knife. Slide it gently between the parchment paper and the side of the pan, loosening all the way along. Then—do your best here, but don't wreck your head—try to bend the palette knife slightly to get it actually under the base of the cake. When you feel you can't get any farther without breaking the cake or starting to cry, call a halt, then use the overhanging edges of the parchment paper as "handles" to lift the entire cake out of the pan. You might have to to-and-fro a little, as in, lift it a bit, then use the palette knife to do a bit more loosening, then lift it a bit more, until it's fully ready to emerge. Peel the paper off, then drizzle the toffee sauce and scatter the peanuts over the top. Cut into thick slices and serve to blokes.

Fridge-Set Honeycomb Cheesecake

The most exciting part of this cheesecake for me was making the honeycomb. Others might not be as excited as me, and may decide to simply go out and buy five Cadbury Crunchies. That's grand. This is a fridge-set cheesecake, which means it's not baked. The setting agent I've used is gelatin, but it isn't suitable for vegetarians, seeing as it's made from cow's hoof or something equally unthinkable. So something else will have to be used. "Agar-agar" is a word I hear bandied about, but I'm afraid I don't know much about it.

Serves 10

For the base

7 ounces homemade honeycomb (which I'll get to)

2 ounces milk chocolate

5 tablespoons butter

OR

5 Cadbury Crunchie bars

5 tablespoons butter

For the honeycomb

¼ cup golden syrup (or substitute dark corn syrup)

¾ cup superfine sugar

3 teaspoons baking soda

For the filling

7 ounces mascarpone cheese

7 ounces Philadelphia cream cheese, at room temperature

¼ cup superfine sugar

¼ cup sweetened condensed milk

1 teaspoon vanilla extract

½ cup heavy cream

2 packets of powdered gelatin

To decorate

edible gold glitter (optional)

To make the honeycomb, grease an 8-inch square baking pan. Put the golden syrup, 1 tablespoon water, and the sugar into a saucepan. Start on a low heat, until the sugar dissolves, then increase. Stir hard. It will really put up a fight at the beginning. Eventually, as it heats up, it will soften. Bring it to a boil, but watch it like a hawk because sugar is notorious for burning. Bring it down to a simmer for 5 to 10 minutes, then add the baking soda and the honeycomb will start foaming like a rabid dog. Stir, for the love of God, stir! The setting process has already started and you're fighting against time to get all the baking soda through before it goes hard. Mix thoroughly, or as thoroughly as you can, and don't get even an atom of it on your skin because this stuff is like napalm.

Pour into your pan, striving for a fairly even height and shape, but it won't be easy. Never mind, you will get to thump it with a mallet later for its misbehavior. It should set in around half an hour, but if it stays sticky and tacky, rather than brittle, put it in the fridge. Block out the rest of your evening in order to wash your saucepan.

To make the base, grease a 9-inch springform pan. If you're using your homemade honeycomb, put it in a plastic bag and shatter it with a mallet (reserve a little for decorating). Melt the chocolate and butter, mix with the honeycomb, then pack into the bottom of the pan and refrigerate for about an hour. Or, if you're using store-bought Crunchies, put them in a plastic bag and bash them to smithereens. Keep approximately one-fifth aside for decorating at the end. Melt the butter, mix with four-fifths of the Crunchies, then pack them into the prepared pan and refrigerate for about an hour. To make the filling, beat the mascarpone, Philadelphia cream cheese, sugar, condensed milk, and vanilla extract. In a separate bowl, beat the cream until it's stiff. Fold the cream into the cheese and sugar mixture.

Prepare the gelatin by pouring 1 cup hot (but not boiling) water into a bowl, then sprinkling the powder on top of the water—the powder always goes into the water, not the other way round. Whisk briskly and for ages—you'll be good and bored—until it's dissolved. Then add it very slowly to the cream cheese mixture. Pour it on top of the set honeycomb base and put in the fridge overnight. Serve with the reserved broken honeycomb and golden glitter sprinkled over the top.

Upside-Down Saffron, Mint, and Pomegranate Cheesecake

Upside-down cheesecakes are really having a moment and it's good to be able to chat knowledgeably about them should they crop up in fashionable conversation, right? Let me guide you through my experience.

The cookie "base" (which will now be on top) can't be as thick as it usually is because the cheesecake will collapse under the weight. So I decided to dispense with cookies altogether and used chopped pistachio nuts instead, which give a gorgeous crunch and a beautiful color. Also, if you normally top your cheesecake with fruit, you have total control over it. But in this case, because the fruit is going *underneath* the cheesecake mixture, it will get cooked and will change during the process. With some fruit (rhubarb, for example) that's a good thing. But, going for a vaguely Middle Eastern theme, I chose pomegranates, visualizing a carpet of ruby-bright red kernels. And in fairness, that's *exactly* what it looked like when I lined the pie dish with them. But by the end of the baking process, they'd gone a pale pink, almost salmony color, which wasn't what I wanted. It still tasted delicious, no harm done, I'm only saying.

Finally, the cheesecake itself didn't set as much as other baked cheesecakes I've made. It became like a thick custard, especially toward the middle, so the best way to serve it is to treat it almost like a trifle. Scoop it out with a big serving spoon, rather than trying to cut it into slices. I realize I might have made this sound like a less than joyous experience, but really it was the opposite. The finished product was a triumph. The subtle strangeness of the saffron worked so well with the sharpness of the mint, and the crunchy sweetness of the pistachio nuts went beautifully with the tang of the pomegranate.

Serves 8–10 people

Pinch of saffron threads

1 cup pomegranate seeds

1 pound mascarpone cheese

2 eggs

¼ cup sour cream

½ cup superfine sugar

2–3 capfuls of mint extract

½ cup all-purpose flour

1 cup shelled pistachio nuts, chopped roughly

I used a 1-quart pie plate, rather than the baking pan I'd usually go for. There's no need to grease it. Preheat the oven to 325°F.

Dissolve the pinch of saffron threads in 2 tablespoons of cold water and set aside. Line the base of your pie plate with your beautiful ruby-red pomegranate seeds. Take a moment to savor their jewel-bright redness because the next time you see them, they'll be a far humbler, more apologetic color.

Beat together the mascarpone, eggs, sour cream, sugar, and mint extract until all the lumps are gone. Add the saffron and the water it was dissolved in—the mixture will go a beautiful yellow color. Sift in the flour and fold through.

Spread the mixture over the pomegranate seeds, trying not to disturb them, if you know what I mean. Try to keep them lining the bottom of the plate, while smoothing the top of the cheesecake mixture to a roughly level finish. But no need to get neurotic about it. Bake for approximately 50 minutes. For the last 20 minutes of cooking, sprinkle the chopped pistachios over.

LIQUID CAKES

Espresso and Walnut Cake

Three Milks Cake (aka A Hug in a Cake)

Rita-Anne's Birthday Cola Cake

Brazilian Stout Cake

Green Tea Panna Cotta

Zaga's Honey Cake

Barmbrack

Coconut Milk Cake

Three Milks Cake (aka A Hug in a Cake)

This is the perfect cake for when you've had a bad shock. Say, like your electricity bill arriving after a hard winter or your credit card bill showing up after a mighty shoe binge. This is a lovely cake—sweet and solid and very comforting. I'd be the first to admit that it doesn't look exciting, and as far as complexity of flavor goes (mere vanilla), it doesn't taste wildly exciting either. But cakes don't always need to be exciting. This is a humble, uncomplicated cake, a very loving cake. If a cake could be described as *kind*, then this is it.

What makes this ordinary cake into something extraordinary are the "three milks." A fairly ordinary sponge cake is soaked in the mix for at least 12 hours, totally transforming the texture and density so that every mouthful is sweet and intense. So what I'm trying to say is, plan ahead. If you know a bad bill is coming on a particular date, make this cake the day before.

Serves 9

1¾ sticks butter

1 cup superfine sugar

4 eggs

1 cup sour cream

Seeds of 1 vanilla pod or
  2 teaspoons vanilla extract

1½ cups self-rising flour

½ teaspoon baking soda

The three milks

1 cup evaporated milk

1 cup sweetened condensed
  milk

1 cup heavy cream

Preheat the oven to 350°F and grease an 8-inch square loose-bottomed pan.

Cream the butter and sugar until pale and fluffy. Add two of the eggs and half of the sour cream and beat well. Add the other two eggs and the rest of the sour cream and beat again. Add the vanilla flavoring, using whichever method you've decided on. Sift in the flour and baking soda and fold into the mixture.

Pile into the prepared pan and bake for approximately 25 minutes, or until a skewer inserted into the middle comes out clean (see page 23).

Cool on a rack until it's fully cooled, but don't take the cake out of the pan. Prick the cake surface several times with a fork. Then—bear with me here, I'll try not to make this sound too complicated—wrap the base of the pan with plastic wrap. What you're trying to do is liquid-proof the pan. Any moment now you'll be pouring in the three milks and you don't want the liquid leaking down the inside of the pan, out through the loose bottom and into your fridge.

Mix the evaporated milk, condensed milk, and cream in a pitcher, then pour it on top of the cake. Most of the liquid will just "sit" on the surface of the cake, but don't be alarmed. Put it in the fridge and over the course of several hours a lot of it will be absorbed.

My experiences with this cake have varied—sometimes nearly all of the milk has disappeared, but other times there's still a milky pool sitting there, looking up at me when I've come to serve it. And the interesting thing is, I've used the exact same quantities every time. If it happens to you that all the liquid doesn't get absorbed, please don't panic, *at all*. Just take a little more care getting it out of the pan, perhaps even using a big serving spoon instead of a knife.

Rita-Anne's Birthday Cola Cake

It was my little sis Rita-Anne's birthday and I decided to make her a cake. I had a good long think about what she likes best (Hula Hoops, which are hollow chip-like potato rings), and I wasn't sure I'd be able to successfully incorporate them into a cake. Then I remembered that she likes cola almost as much as Hula Hoops, so I made this and she was delighted.

Serves 12–14

1 cup (2 sticks) butter, at room temperature

1½ cups brown sugar

2 eggs

2 teaspoons vanilla extract

1 cup cola*

½ cup buttermilk

2 cups self-rising flour

⅓ cup cocoa powder

1 teaspoon baking soda

4 cups mini marshmallows

For the icing

⅓ cup cola

½ cup (1 stick) butter

3 tablespoons cocoa powder

2 cups confectioners' sugar

a bag of fizzy cola bottles (optional)

*Any brand will do, but it must not be sugar-free or diet, you need the sugar from it.

Preheat the oven to 350°F. Grease and line a big baking pan, 12 inches by 9 inches and 2 inches deep, with parchment paper. If you're thinking that this is a BIG cake, big and flat, you're right. It's called a "sheet" cake.

Beat the butter with the sugar until creamy. Add the eggs and vanilla extract. Mix the cola and buttermilk together in a pitcher. In a bowl, mix the flour, cocoa powder, and baking soda together.

Pour about a third of the cola and buttermilk mixture into the creamed butter and sugar, then sift in about a third of the flour/cocoa/soda mixture and stir well. Add another third of the liquid, then another third of the flour and stir again. Go again and it'll all be in. When it's blended and smooth, stir in the marshmallows.

Pour into your—frankly, massive-looking—baking sheet and bake for about 35 to 40 minutes. Do the Skewer Test (see page 23). One thing to note, during the baking process the marshmallows will melt, causing small craters to appear in your cake. This is *fine*, you have done nothing wrong. The melted marshmallows will regroup into little, dense, sticky spots of deliciousness, popping up unexpectedly and giving texture and surprise.

Cool the cake on a rack, then extract it from the pan. Proceed with caution because the cake is so big and unwieldy.

To make the icing, put the cola, butter, and cocoa powder into a largeish saucepan and heat until the butter is melted. Bring to a boil, stirring constantly. Take off the heat, sift in the confectioners' sugar, and whisk like mad. Give this everything you've got because even when you think all of the confectioners' sugar is incorporated, I can assure you it isn't. Stubborn little cysts of it will hold out for an *astonishingly* long time. As the renegade lumps are reluctantly flushed out, the icing will thicken. Eventually you can stop. Let it cool and thicken a little.

If you like, you can simply spread the icing over the cake as it is, in all its enormous, never-ending, prairie-like glory. Or you can cut the cake in half and stack one piece on top of the other, sandwiching them with half the icing, then spreading the remaining icing over the top and sides. Finally, decorate with fizzy cola bottles.

Brazilian Stout Cake

Have you been to Brazil? It's the most wonderful place, with the loveliest people, and I loved the food so much that I bought myself a Brazilian cookbook (called, with admirable straightforwardness, *Brazilian Cookery*). I was particularly interested in the cake recipes, but there were some I couldn't make because the ingredients were so exotic—manioc root, anyone?—but this one, with its main ingredient of stout, e.g., Guinness (or similar brand), couldn't have been easier.

I'll address your reservations right now by saying, don't worry about the Guinness. You don't really taste it at all, you just get an intriguing, dark undertow. Also, the alcohol evaporates, so it's okay to give it to everyone.

I used lemon buttercream icing and found its sharpness cut through the malty, molassesy cake with flair and aplomb.

You'll notice in the photo that this cake has three layers. I only intended to have two layers, but I accidentally poured far more cake mixture into one pan than the other, so that one cake layer ended up almost twice as thick as the other. It was all a bit embarrassing until Himself came up with the idea of slicing the big piece in half horizontally, giving me three layers, almost all the same size. If you also want to go for the three layers, consider doubling the icing.

Serves 12–14

½ cup (1 stick) butter
½ cup brown sugar
4 eggs, separated
½ teaspoon ground ginger
1 teaspoon ground cinnamon
1 teaspoon ground mace*
1 tablespoon grated lemon zest
2¼ cups all-purpose flour
½ teaspoon salt
1 tablespoon baking powder
1 cup stout
¾ cup molasses
1 teaspoon baking soda

For the icing

1⅓ sticks butter
2½ cups confectioners' sugar
1 teaspoon lemon juice
yellow food coloring (optional)

Preheat the oven to 350°F and grease two 9-inch cake pans.

Cream the butter and sugar. Beat the egg yolks with the ginger, cinnamon, mace, and lemon zest. Add to the butter/sugar mixture. In a bowl, mix the flour, salt, and baking powder together.

Heat the beer to lukewarm and mix in the molasses and baking soda. Sift a third of the flour mixture into the eggs/butter/sugar, then a third of the beer/molasses. Combine well. Add another third of each and stir again. Add the final third.

Stiffly beat the egg whites and fold into the mixture. Divide—equally!—between your two pans. Bake for 35 minutes. Do the Skewer Test (see page 23), then turn out of the pans onto wire racks. Leave to cool.

Make the icing by creaming together the butter and sugar, then adding the lemon juice and enough food coloring until you get your desired yellowness. Use the icing to sandwich the cake layers together, then spread over the top of the cake and down the sides.

*Not the stuff you spray in muggers' eyes. It might sound strange and scary, but it's from the same plant as nutmeg. You can substitute nutmeg if necessary.

Green Tea Panna Cotta

Panna Cotta (Italian for "cooked cream") is the simplest, most delicious thing ever. The ingredients are basically cream, milk, sugar, flavoring, and a setting agent. As with the Fridge-Set Honeycomb Cheesecake recipe on page 91, the setting agent I've used is gelatin, which isn't suitable for vegetarians. My apologies for that, but I believe agar-agar will fit your needs.

However, what I really want to talk to you about is the flavoring. People balked a little when I told them what they were getting—green tea seems to have a fairly joyless rep—but they became a lot more enthusiastic and animated when I withheld the info about the flavoring. These panna cotta really taste amazing—subtle, delicate, intriguing, and delightful.

It seems to be the done thing to make panna cotta in small individual containers. I'm the lucky owner of four adorable little silicone molds that look like old-fashioned blancmanges. But you can use anything really—ramekins, cups, square sauce bowls, disposable plastic glasses that you get wine in at office leaving parties, etc.—so long as they have a capacity of about 1 cup.

Serves 4

2½ cups heavy cream
½ cup whole milk
⅔ cup superfine sugar
12 green tea bags
1 packet powdered
  gelatin
edible glitter (optional)

In a heavy saucepan, bring the cream, milk, and sugar to a boil and keep it boiling for about 4 minutes. Lower the temperature, add the tea bags, and simmer for 2 to 3 minutes, stirring regularly.

Take the saucepan off the heat and leave to cool for about 5 minutes—it's important that the liquid is below boiling point when you add the gelatin. Remove the tea bags and discard them. Then, whisking very briskly with a hand whisk, add the gelatin. Remember that the powder always gets poured on top of the liquid, never the other way round, and make sure that the gelatin is fully dissolved—this could take a good few minutes of tedious whisking—before you proceed to the next stage. Pour the mixture into the molds and leave to set in the fridge for at least 3 hours.

To be quite honest, the trickiest part of making this beautiful dessert is getting it out. What I do is I run a little hot water over the bottom of each mold, then gently run the tip of a small sharp knife completely around the edge of the mould, just a few millimeters below the surface. I patiently ease the panna cotta away from the sides and when I feel I can't go any farther without breaking the panna cotta, I upend the mold onto the serving bowl and—again more patience required, and I'm so bad at it—"peel" the mold off.

If you're not using a flexible mold, a tip I got from the Interweb is to slide your small sharp knife down as far as you can and simultaneously tip the mold onto its side over the serving dish. Apparently the knife down the side creates an air pocket and helps the panna cotta pop right out onto the dish.

Another extra-special handy hint I came across is to have a droplet of water in the middle of your serving bowl or plate so that if your panna cotta comes out and lands off-center, you can slide it around until it's centered.

Zaga's Honey Cake

Zaga is mother-in-law to my brother Niall, who is married to Zaga's daughter Ljiljana. Zaga lives in Belgrade and is an AMAZING cook, producing absolute feasts from a (Christ, I hope she won't mind me saying this) tiny kitchen. This cake is straightforward, simple, and delicious.

My instinct is always to add tons of spicing and flavoring (often to the point where people choke), but there's no need here, the honey is flavory enough. Indeed, did you know that the kind of honey you use will influence the taste? I'd always thought honey was just honey, but not at all, there's a universe of different kinds out there. Apparently, it all depends on the kinds of flowers the bees are getting their pollen from. Isn't nature amazing?

Makes 16 cubes

5 eggs, separated

½ cup superfine sugar

½ cup oil (sunflower, walnut, or hazelnut, if you can get it)

½ cup honey

1½ cups all-purpose flour

2 teaspoons baking powder

2 ounces nuts (walnuts, almonds, hazelnuts), finely chopped*

To decorate

edible gold shimmer (optional)

* Feel free to use whatever you like—I used hazelnuts.

Preheat the oven to 400°F and prepare an 8-inch square pan by brushing with oil, then dusting with flour.

Beat the egg yolks with the sugar, then add the oil, honey, flour, baking powder, and nuts. In a separate bowl, beat the egg whites until stiff. Mix the two lots together—the yolk mixture will be quite stiff and resistant and the challenge is to fold in the egg whites without knocking all the air out. Do your best, but don't wreck your head.

Pour the mixture into your prepared pan, put into the oven, and reduce the temperature to 350°F. Bake for 25 to 30 minutes, or until a skewer comes out clean (see page 23).

Cool on a rack, then cut into cubes. If you'd like, you can brush with edible gold shimmer, but there's no need to do anything if you don't want. These little cubes look quite innocuous, but they're lovely. The honey flavor comes as an excellent surprise.

Barmbrack

I'm fairly sure this is an Irish thing. It's traditionally served as a Halloween sweetmeat, but you won't be arrested if you serve it at another time of the year. Except for the month of May. (I joke, of course.)

Basically Barmbrack is a simple loaf cake where the main ingredient is black tea, but with a charming twist—little "gifts" are dotted in it at random. Common examples are a ring, a key, a coin, and a small piece of wood. (The idea goes that if you get the ring in your slice you'll be getting married; a key means a new home or maybe a new car; cracking your tooth on the coin indicates that you'll be coming into money, which will come in handy for paying the dentist; and if you end up with the stick, it means that you'll remain a spinster—delightful.)

Feel free to improvise with your own "surprises"—for example, I've sometimes added a Berocca vitamin tablet to guarantee good health; hair clips to ward off male-pattern baldness; or a tiny little shoe to predict ... er ... well, new shoes. But for the love of God, wrap each "surprise" in a big lump of aluminum foil, to make them unmissably visible so that no one accidentally swallows them. People have gone terrible litigious.

Serves 8–10

¾ cup light brown sugar
½ cup golden raisins
½ cup raisins
1½ ounces citrus peel
2 cups black tea, cooled
1¼ cups self-rising flour
1 level teaspoon baking soda
1 egg, beaten

Put the sugar, fruit, peel, and tea in a bowl. Leave to soak overnight.

On the day itself, grease a 1-pound loaf pan and line it with parchment paper OR save yourself all that trouble and use a silicone loaf pan. Preheat the oven to 325°F.

Sift the flour and baking soda into the tea/sugar/fruit stew, then add the beaten egg and stir well.

Pour into your loaf pan, then "plant" your little surprises at regular intervals into the mix so that each slice will contain something and you don't have anyone boohoohooing and bellyaching and saying that they didn't get anything and that their younger brother is going to be getting a Ferrari and why do they never get anything and why is life so unfair. Make sure that each piece of foil is fully immersed in the cake mixture because if it's sticking up into the open air, it might burn. Bake for 1 hour and 35 minutes or do your Skewer Test (see page 23).

Leave for 5 minutes, then turn out onto a wire rack. Cut into slices and serve with plenty of butter. Because of the foil-wrapped surprises, this is a very sociable cake, one of the few that I like to share with others. (In a perfect universe, I'd prefer to eat cake alone, in a darkened room, answerable to no one, slice after slice. And when it's all gone, I'd brush off any incriminating crumbs, fold the box into very small pieces, stash it in the bottom of the bin, and deny that there had ever been any baked goods in the house at all.)

PASTRY. Scares the life out of people. Almost as bad as meringues. But don't be afraid. I'll hold your hand through this.

Nearly all the recipes I'll take you through are versions of shortcrust pastry—I've started with a basic recipe and become progressively more ambitious and fancy. (There is a short, terrifying detour, where we'll veer wildly off track and do choux pastry, but then we'll return to the path.) We're going to make a couple of dishes using puff pastry and filo pastry, but we're not even going to attempt to make the pastry because everyone—even, I'm reliably informed, professional chefs—buys the pre-made stuff. If they cannot be bothered to make it from scratch, I don't see why we should put ourselves through it. There is no shame in this.

The key to good shortcrust pastry is to keep everything as cold as possible. Professional bakers make their pastry in the morning, before the kitchen heats up. I mean, that's the level of sensitivity we're dealing with here.

Most of the recipes I'm giving you here are pie *bases*, so the pastry is playing a mere supporting part, rather than a leading role. Just a quick note—I've baked them in pie plates or dishes rather than cake pans. They're very similar but with a pie plate or dish the side will gently slope outward. Sometimes the sides will be "fluted," which means frilly. Also—sorry to bamboozle you with details—pie plates come in different depths. Shallow ones are about 1¼ inches deep and deeper ones can be 2 inches deep, but I'm only using shallow ones in this section.

Mini Key Lime Pies

These little beauties are made with a basic shortcrust pastry, as basic as it gets. It's basically flour, butter, and water, nothing to scare the horses.

In keeping with this gentle introduction, these pies are small, which means there's less surface area of pastry to grapple with, which, trust me, helps a lot.

Just one thing, these need to be refrigerated for at least 6 hours, so plan ahead.

Makes 4 mini pies

For the basic shortcrust pastry

1⅓ cups all-purpose flour

pinch of salt

7 tablespoons butter, chilled and cut into cubes

For the filling

4 egg yolks

1¾ cups sweetened condensed milk

juice of 6 limes

To decorate

edible glitter and lime slices (optional)

For these pies, I use 4 silicone molds, 4½ inches wide. Because I use silicone molds, there's no need to grease them. But if you're using metal pans, butter liberally.

There are a couple of ways we can make shortcrust pastry—by hand or by machine. In the next recipe I'll tell you the food processor method, but here I'm going to tell you how to make pastry by hand. You might think, For the love of God, I've got a busy life, I've better things to be doing than making pastry by hand! Or you might think, I'm going out of my mind here, give me some sort of small, soothing task. And really, this is as small and soothing as it gets.

Sift the flour and salt into a bowl, then add the cubed butter. Using the tips of your fingers, start rubbing small pieces of butter and small pieces of flour together. As you do, lift your hands into the air above the bowl and let the stuff fall back in. Eventually—but it'll take a while—the mixture will begin to resemble fine breadcrumbs.

Don't try to speed this up. If you do it too quickly, the butter will become greasy and your pastry won't be as crisp. So slow down. Embrace the process. Think of it as meditation for your fingers.

Remember what I said about coldness. Think about Lapland. Blizzards. Frostbite.

Keep rubbing and lifting and breathing and feeling your feet on the ground and when you feel the flour and butter have become as one, add a tablespoon of cold water and—mark me carefully here—stir it in using a knife. Yes, a knife. I had always been told that it was bad luck to stir anything with a knife, but now I feel there's no such thing as good or bad luck, life is simply life and we can't ward off bad stuff by saluting magpies or lighting candles or refusing to stir things with knives. Whatever is going to happen is going to happen, so stir away. The knife will keep things cold, so even if the roof falls in, your pastry will be nice. •••

The mixture will start to cohere, by that I mean it'll start sticking together and looking like pastry. If you need to add another tablespoon of water, do, but easy does it, you don't want your pastry to become tacky. Use your hands for the final "bringing together."

Pat it into a flat round, cover in plastic wrap, and put in the fridge for at least an hour.

Now it's time to roll out your pastry and there are a couple of ways we can do this. We'll do the Floured Surface Version here and I'll tell you the Plastic Wrap Method in the next recipe.

First, preheat the oven to 325°F.

Remove the plastic wrap and with a sharp knife, cut the pastry into quarters.

Dust a clean surface with flour and place one of the quarters of pastry in the middle of it. Also dust your rolling pin with flour (unless you have a non-stick silicone one) and with firm, confident strokes, flatten and "stretch" the pastry so that it becomes more of an oval shape. Shift the pastry 90 degrees so that now it's wide and short. Sweep a fresh layer of flour under the pastry because otherwise it will stick to the surface and it'll be a nightmare. Roll again and now you'll have more of a round shape. Keep shifting the pastry 90 degrees, keep sweeping fresh flour under the pastry and keep rolling, until the dough is big enough and roughly the right shape to line the bottom and sides of one of your molds. This shouldn't take long because the molds are small and it'll be a different story when we're dealing with full-sized pies, but let's not worry about that now.

Trim the edge of the pastry with a sharp knife and bake the pastry blind for 15 minutes (see page 21).

To make the filling, whisk the egg yolks until they go a little pale. Add in the condensed milk and the juice of the 6 limes, then whisk again. Divide the mixture among the four partially baked pastry shells and bake for 15 minutes.

Cool on a wire rack and refrigerate for at least 6 hours.

If you're in the mood, decorate with glitter and other stuff, but they're just as wonderful served plain.

Mam's Apple Tart

Mam is my beloved mother. A famously reluctant cook, she was, however, a dab hand at the apple tarts and could make them in her sleep. This is utterly delicious and brought memories of childhood rushing back.

Serves 6

For the pastry

1⅓ cups all-purpose flour

½ cup confectioners' sugar

½ cup (1 stick) butter, chilled and cut into cubes

1 egg yolk

For the filling

5 baking apples, peeled, cored, and chopped

4 cloves and 1 cinnamon stick*

2 tablespoons superfine sugar

For the glaze

1 egg, lightly beaten (or milk)

superfine sugar

*Obviously my mother didn't use such stuff. Any Irish woman found adding flavoring to food in the 1960s could have been stripped of her citizenship.

Grease an 8-inch pie plate.

You can make this pastry in your food processor if you're lucky enough to have one. (If not, see the instructions in the previous recipe for making pastry by hand.) Sift the flour and confectioners' sugar together, then add the butter. Beat slowly until the mixture goes sandy and there are no lumps of butter still visible. Add the egg yolk and mix again. The pastry should gradually cohere, i.e., start looking like pastry. If it still looks dry and crumbly (this is unlikely) add a tablespoon of cold water and mix again.

Wrap the lump of pastry in plastic wrap, then put in the fridge for at least an hour.

Meanwhile, put the chopped baking apples into a heavy-bottomed saucepan. (To be quite honest, I didn't know you could even *get* baking apples anymore. I thought they were something from the olden days.)

Bash the cloves (this releases their oil) and add to the apples along with the cinnamon stick. Add the superfine sugar and 2 tablespoons water and stew over a gentle heat. However, to quote Mam here, "Go aisy! You don't want the apples to turn to mush."

When the apples are soft but still lumpy—this should take about 20 minutes—test for sweetness. If you think they're a bit sour, add more sugar.

Preheat the oven to 325°F.

Now, for the Plastic Wrap Method of rolling out pastry. Take the pastry out of the fridge and remove the plastic wrap. Divide the pastry into two "halves," one slightly bigger than the other. Shape the bigger half into a round, then place on a piece of plastic wrap, about 12 inches by 12 inches. Place another piece of plastic wrap—roughly the same size as the first one—on top of the pastry, then use your rolling pin to flatten the pastry. To confirm, your pastry is enveloped between both pieces of plastic wrap and your rolling pin is rolling over the top piece. I'm sorry if this is confusing. The thing is, it's actually a useful thing to get the hang of because the plastic wrap will "hold" the pastry so that it's less likely to break as you roll it out. •••

So roll the pastry, then turn the whole plastic-wrapped parcel 90 degrees and roll again, and so on, until your pastry is roughly the right size and shape to line your pan. You might think, Feck this plastic wrap malarkey, it's far too much trouble, and if so, then stop. I don't want to add to your woes, only reduce them.

Right, now the tricky bit, getting the pastry into the pan. Remove the top layer of plastic wrap. Place your rolling pin horizontally across the dough and using it almost as a hinge, fold the pastry in two and lift it off the bottom layer of plastic wrap—do this *very* quickly, this is not a time to start staring thoughtfully into the distance and musing on existential matters—then lower it into the pan.

Things might go pear-shaped on you—they did for me, my pastry "broke"—but don't panic. What I did was assemble a "patchwork" pastry shell. I put the biggest unbroken piece into the pan, then used the next-biggest piece to cover more of the pan, overlapping the edges slightly. I kept doing this until the pan was fully lined, then I pressed my fingers along the edges until they had all but disappeared.

Even if your pastry doesn't fully break, holes may develop and there's no shame in this, no shame at all. Just patch the holes with more pastry and move on.

Trim the edges with a sharp knife, then add in the stewed apple. Yes, that's right, no baking blind on this tart. Mam sounded *extremely* surprised when I suggested it. She's never done it—probably because she was so busy—but the tarts never suffered. It means that the bottom layer of pastry stays soft and crumbly, instead of crunchy, but no less delicious for it.

Roll out the second "half" of pastry using whichever method appeals to you, then drape it over the top of the tart. Stick the edge of the bottom layer against the edge of the top layer, using the egg wash or milk.

Swipe the top layer with the egg wash or milk and prick several times with a fork. Bake for about 30 minutes, until the pastry is golden brown.

Scatter superfine sugar over the top just before serving.

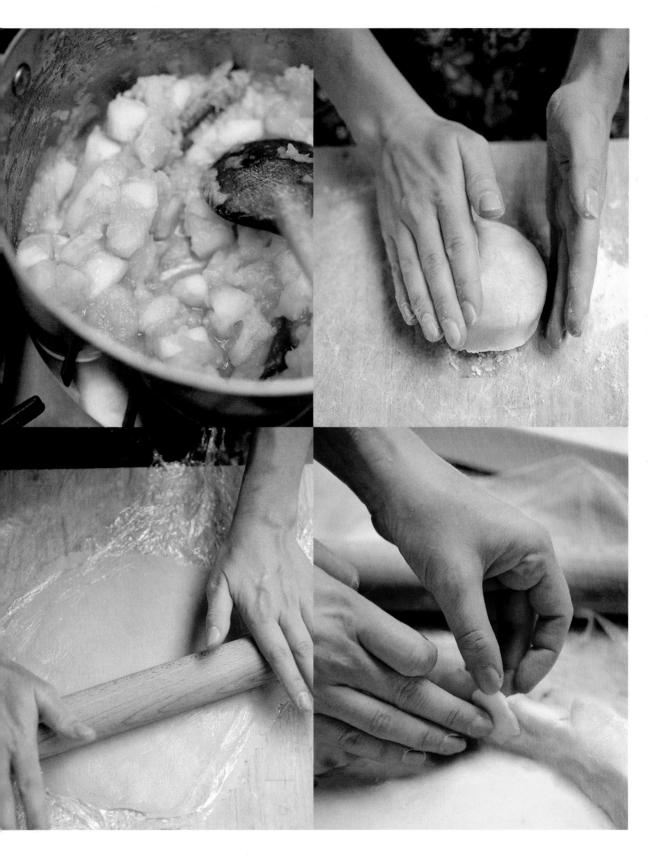

Pecan Pie

Now, *this* is a magnificent creation. It's a pastry base, with a pecan nut and golden syrup filling, topped off by serried ranks of perfect pecans, made extra beautiful-looking with the addition of a glaze.

Serves 10

For the pastry

1¾ cups all-purpose flour

pinch of salt

2 ounces lard, chilled and cut into cubes*

6 tablespoons (¾ stick) butter, chilled and cut into cubes

2 teaspoons superfine sugar

For the filling

4 cups pecans

3 eggs

1 cup light brown sugar

⅔ cup golden syrup (or substitute dark corn syrup)

3½ tablespoons butter, melted

1 teaspoon vanilla extract

2 tablespoons all-purpose flour

For the (optional) glaze

2 tablespoons pear/apple spread**

*I know! Sounds gross, yes? But go with it.

**You can get it in health food shops.

Grease a 9-inch pie plate.

Make the pastry by sifting the flour into a bowl with the salt and rubbing the fat in, either using your hands or your food processor. When the mixture starts to look like fine breadcrumbs, add the sugar. At this stage you might be able to bring the pastry together with your hands. If it still looks a bit crumbly, add a tablespoon of cold water. Now, with this pie, I did something a little unexpected (even to myself). I didn't chill the pastry and then roll it out. I shaped the pastry into a ball, placed it in the center of the dish, and used the heel of my hand to flatten it. I kept pushing and flattening the pastry until it reached the edges of the dish, then encouraged it to climb the sides. In fairness, things got a little lopsided, with one side a bit thicker than the other, but no matter! I simply removed a strip of pastry from the "fat" side and use it to bulk out the thinner side.

When the entire inside of the pan was lined with pastry, I put it in the fridge for half an hour.

When the half hour was up, I preheated the oven to 400°F and baked the pastry blind for 20 minutes (see page 21). Then I removed the paper and beans and baked it for another 5 minutes.

Meanwhile, I began the filling by segregating the pecans, keeping the handsome, whole ones aside for decorating the top and shunting off the manky, broken ones for inclusion in the mixture. I didn't feel good about this pecan nut apartheid and resolved that the next time, the broken ones would be on display.

I whisked the eggs, then added the sugar, golden syrup, melted butter, vanilla extract, sifted flour, and reject pecans, stirring well. I poured the mixture into the pastry shell and arranged the good-looking pecans in an attractive fashion on the top.

At this point, I lowered the oven temperature to 325°F and baked for about a further 30 minutes. (Cover with a bit of aluminum foil if the pecans on top begin to burn.)

While the tart cooled (on a wire rack) I mixed the apple/pear spread with 2 tablespoons of boiling water and microwaved on half power for 2 minutes, then used a pastry brush to paint the glaze over the top.

Pear and Hazelnut Flan

What makes this flan extra special is the addition of ground hazelnuts into the pastry. It gives an unexpected density of flavor, which goes very nicely with the sweetness of the pears. This flan might seem like a very work-intensive thing because you'll be making custard and a glaze in addition to the pastry, but it's all fairly simple and very worth it.

Serves 10

For the pastry

⅓ cup hazelnuts, ground to a fine flour

¾ cup all-purpose flour

pinch of salt

5 tablespoons butter, chilled and cut into cubes

1 tablespoon superfine sugar

1 egg, beaten

For the filling

3 eggs

1 egg yolk

¼ cup superfine sugar

1 teaspoon vanilla extract

1¼ cups heavy cream

3–4 ripe pears, peeled, halved, and cored

For the glaze

4 tablespoons apricot jam

Grease an 8- or 9-inch flan dish.

Make the pastry by mixing the ground nuts, sifted flour, and salt, then incorporating the butter using either your fingers or your food processor. When the mixture resembles fine breadcrumbs, add the sugar, then make a well in the middle and add the beaten egg. It should start looking like pastry at this stage, but if it's still a bit dry, add a tablespoon of cold water.

Roll the pastry into a ball, wrap in plastic wrap, and refrigerate for an hour.

When the hour is nearly up, preheat the oven to 350°F. (Any pastry made with nuts needs to be cooked at a slightly lower temperature than plain pastry, because the nuts are more prone to burning.) Roll the pastry out using your preferred method (see page 117 for the Floured Surface version or page 119 for the Plastic Wrap Method), bake blind for 15 minutes (see page 21), then remove the paper and beans and bake for another 10 minutes.

Meanwhile, make the custard filling by whipping the eggs, the egg yolk, the sugar, and the vanilla extract, but not for long, you're not looking for foamy here, just mixed. Scald the cream (see page 21), then *very, very gradually* pour it into the beaten eggs, whisking all the time. (The reason you add it so gradually is to prevent the heat of the cream from scrambling the eggs.)

Pour the custard into your pastry shell, then place the pear halves, spaced at equal intervals, into the custard. Back into the oven it goes for another 30 minutes, but keep an eye on it. If the edges of the pastry start to look like they might take a notion to be overcooked—or, God forbid, even burnt—cover the whole thing with a sheet of aluminum foil.

Cool on a wire rack and make the glaze by adding a tablespoon of boiling water to the apricot jam, then microwaving on half power for 2 minutes. Strain the warm jam through a sieve so that the fruity "bits" get left behind and what goes into your bowl is a sticky liquid.

Use a pastry brush to gently paste the glaze on to the surface of the flan. This makes a HUGE difference to the final look of the flan—it's like the difference between going out without your lipstick on, and with it on. HUGE difference.

Chocolate Hazelnut Torte

We're stepping things up a further notch here by making chocolate pastry. Not as intimidating to make as it might initially sound because the chocolatey-ness is coming from cocoa powder rather than melted chocolate. The filling, on the other hand, is a stunningly rich, delicious affair. Chocolate and hazelnuts are a great combination and some strange witchcraft happens when you add coffee. Instead of making the torte taste like coffee, it has the effect of making the chocolate taste even more like chocolate. And God knows, that has to be good.

Serves 8

For the chocolate pastry

1½ cups all-purpose flour

½ cup cocoa powder

½ teaspoon baking powder

¼ cup confectioners' sugar

10 tablespoons butter, chilled and cut into cubes

3 egg yolks

For the filling

5½ ounces dark chocolate (70% cocoa solids)

10 tablespoons butter

⅔ cup superfine sugar

5 ounces hazelnuts, ground to a fine flour

4 eggs, separated

⅓ cup cocoa powder

1 tablespoon instant coffee, dissolved in 2 tablespoons boiling water, then cooled

Liberally grease an 8- or 9-inch pie plate with butter, but don't go preheating any oven yet, hold your horses!

Make the pastry by sifting together the flour, cocoa powder, and baking powder. Add the confectioners' sugar, then incorporate the butter, either by using your fingers or using your food processor. When it starts to look like fine breadcrumbs, add in the egg yolks. It should become quite sticky at this stage.

Because of its wet consistency, this pastry is quite tricky to handle, so my advice is that you don't roll it out with a rolling pin, but that you use the Pressing Method I described on page 122. I promise you it'll make life much easier.

When the pie plate is fully lined, put it in the fridge and chill for at least 20 minutes.

Preheat the oven to 400°F and bake the pastry blind for 15 minutes (see page 21). Then remove the beans and paper and bake for another 5 minutes.

Take the pastry out of the oven and reduce the temperature to 325°F.

Now it's time to make the fabulous filling.

Melt the chocolate and butter together in a large heatproof bowl over a saucepan of simmering water.

Remove from the heat and beat in the sugar, ground hazelnuts, egg yolks, cocoa powder, and dissolved coffee.

In a separate bowl, beat the egg whites until they're holding soft peaks, then fold into the chocolate mixture.

Pour into the pastry shell and bake for 40 minutes—when you take it out, the middle will probably still have a bit of wobble to it, this is all fine—and cool on a wire rack.

Remove with great care from the plate and serve in smallish slices because this is very, very intense and you don't want your guests (or indeed yourself) going into a chocolate coma.

Lemon Curd and Pistachio Pinwheels

This is another fabulous recipe where you barefacedly use store-bought puff pastry.

Makes 16

a packet of 2 sheets of
  frozen prepared puff
  pastry, total weight
  1 pound*

For the filling

6 ounces lemon curd

1½ cups pistachios,
  chopped roughly

*The ones I bought came
  rolled up so, while they
  were still frozen, I unrolled
  them and laid them flat.
  They each came on a
  sheet of plastic (blue, if
  it's of any interest), so I
  just kept them on it and
  didn't have to bother with
  floured boards. I gave them
  about an hour and a half to
  defrost.

Line two baking sheets with parchment paper and preheat the oven to 425°F.

Spread half of the lemon curd onto the first pastry sheet—it should be a very thin covering, a mere scraping—then scatter over half of the pistachios. Take the short end of the pastry, lift it slightly, and start rolling it inward and over onto itself, as tightly as possible, but not so tightly that the filling starts to squeeze out the sides. (This gets easier with practice, I promise.) Proceed with patience but confidence, making sure that the rolling is happening evenly across the width of the pastry.

Very soon, it will be all rolled up and you will have a little log.

Repeat the whole process with the second sheet of pastry and the rest of the lemon curd and pistachios.

Use a serrated knife to cut each log into eight equal pieces. You might have to dip the knife in water occasionally because the lemon curd filling may stick to it and make the cutting difficult. Carefully lay each pinwheel flat on your baking sheets. Leave plenty of room between them because the pastry will puff and expand.

Bake for about 20 minutes. There might be mild filling leakage from some of the pinwheels, but don't let that bother you. Do watch though that they don't burn on the bottom.

When you take the pinwheels out of the oven, prepare to be amazed. They will look so professional and impressive and totally different from the last time you saw them.

Let them stay on their sheets while they cool.

You can re-create this with a million different fillings—morello cherry jam and chopped hazelnuts, for example. Or lime curd—have you ever had the pleasure? Very hard to get hold of, but oh my God, SO delicious, far nicer than lemon, if you ask me—teamed with chopped macadamia nuts. Let your imagination run wild! But *never* lie about the pastry being store-bought.

Chocolate Baklava

This is another shame-free recipe using more store-bought pastry, filo this time. Baklava, though. Cripes, was I intimidated. So intimidated that I had to involve Himself because he has a lot of qualities that I lack—patience, dexterity, and patience. Also, he's very patient. (I defensively describe myself as more of an "ideas" person.) So using our different but symbiotic personalities, we fashioned a Baklava together and I swear to God, we were so proud of the finished product that it was almost like we'd had a baby. We kept taking photos of it, the way people do with newborns.

In one way I was right to be so intimidated—filo pastry is very fragile and large sheets of it are hard to handle without them tearing. But next time I think I could do it on my own. I'll take you through it step-by-step so that you can do this solo if you want.

The Nutella was my idea (did I mention that I'm an "ideas" person?).

Makes about 20 baklava, approx. 4 cm by 5 cm

For the baklava
12 sheets of uncooked
  and defrosted filo pastry*
2 cups pistachios
2 cups walnuts
1 cup pecans
6 cardamom pods
6 ounces Nutella
12 tablespoons (1½ sticks)
  butter

For the syrup
1¼ cups granulated sugar
2 capfuls of rosewater

*The only filo pastry sheets I could find were exactly the right width for my baking pan, but too long. I agonized about what to do with the excess and couldn't come up with a solution, so I'm afraid there was some wastage. You might have better luck finding shorter sheets. Or you might have a longer pan.

You'll be using a 9-inch by 12-inch baking pan. Preheat the oven to 350°F.

Have the pastry standing by, but keep it covered with a damp cloth as it dries out quickly.

Make the filling by putting all the nuts and the cardamom pods into a food processor and grinding them until they're pretty small. Not complete dust, but say, the size of large breadcrumbs. Move them to a separate bowl, add the Nutella, and mix well. Keep standing by.

Melt the butter until it's liquid. Using a pastry brush, paint a lot of melted butter on the base and up the sides of the pan you're using. Then, this is where it could get challenging. Take a sheet of filo pastry and gently lay it on the base of the pan. Carefully brush it with melted butter, then take another length of pastry, lay it on top of the first one, and brush with melted butter. Keep going, until you've got six slices of filo pastry, lying one on top of the other, with a layer of melted butter in between each.

Remember, the pastry is very thin and fragile. Himself was in charge of draping and laying and I was in charge of brushing the melted butter and it was fairly intensive work. At one stage Himself said, "Imagine if you had to actually *make* the filo pastry as well as all this other stuff." He had a good think about it and then he muttered, "God, no *wonder* the Ottoman Empire collapsed."

When the six layers are in place, spread the nut/cardamom/Nutella evenly over the entire surface. Then it's time to start preparing the "top" of your baklava. Lay a length of pastry over the nut/Nutella

•••

mixture, brush with melted butter, lay down another layer of pastry, again brushing with melted butter, and so on until you've used up all the pastry. (All in all, you should have used twelve sheets of pastry, six underneath the filling and six on top.) Finish with a layer of melted butter.

Then it's time to cut the baklava into shapes—it's easier to do this now than later when they're cooked. It's traditional to serve baklava in diamond shapes and the best way to do this is to first cut the uncooked baklava in the pan into four long, equally sized strips (going right down to the bottom layer of pastry). Then cut diagonal lines—the more lines you cut, the smaller your individual baklava will be. Himself cut approximately five diagonal lines, which ended up giving us twenty pieces, but if you cut more lines, closer to each other, you'll get more—but smaller—cakes.

Bake for 20 minutes, then lower the temperature to 300°F and cook for another 30 to 40 minutes.

Meanwhile, make the syrup by dissolving the sugar in 1¼ cups water and the rosewater. Stirring constantly, bring it to bubbling point, but make sure it doesn't burn. Leave to cool.

When the baklava comes out of the oven, go over the diagonal cuts again with a sharp knife, then pour the syrup along the "fault lines." Leave the baklava to absorb the syrup for a good few hours, overnight if possible. This is a stunningly delicious cake and people simply won't be able to believe that you made it yourself.

MERINGUES AND MACARONS

Blueberry Mess

Shirley's Ginger and Pineapple Pavlova

Zagina Reforma Torta (Zaga's Reform Chocolate Cake)

Banana Meringue Pie

Basic Cranberry Macarons

Mango Macarons

Apple Macarons

Bluegrass Macarons

Tiramisu Macarons

Very Chocolatey Macarons

People fear **MERINGUES**. They regard the egg white as a slippery customer—unreliable, capricious, even treacherous. And I agree that an egg white has to be handled right. But there is a key to mastering meringues and that key is to be just a little OCD—have your bowl super-clean, have your beaters super-clean (not that they'd be any other way, of course) and separate your eggs with extreme care—don't let even an atom of egg yolk get into the egg whites (which is why I recommend using three bowls, see the tip on page 21). The thing is, that grease of any kind is the enemy of the meringue. I won't bamboozle you with the science, but basically grease *interferes*. It stops the egg whites from becoming foamy and thick, so you could be beating until Judgment Day and your egg whites could still be eyeballing you with mulish resistance, refusing to change.

Apparently, there's also a danger of overbeating egg whites and causing the mix to curdle. However, that's never happened to me because I have too short an attention span and get bored long before we reach that point.

The best bowl to make meringues in is copper—a chemical reaction happens that stabilizes the egg whites—but I don't have a copper bowl and I've still managed to produce the goods, so don't stress.

From my experience, there are several versions of meringues and a lot has to do with the temperature and length of time they're baked at. You get meringues that are dry, crunchy, almost chalky. Then there are "cakey" meringues, which are made with a high quantity of ground nuts. Sometimes meringue is used as a pie topping so that it's golden on the outside but still "wet" on the inside. Or you can have meringues that are downright chewy, as in **MACARONS**. They are all fabulous.

Blueberry Mess

A nice easy introduction to meringues, this one. Very simple. It's a variation on the classic Eton Mess, only I've used blueberries instead of strawberries and Greek yogurt instead of cream. And you don't have to have gone to Eton.

There's very little that can go wrong here. This is a "dry" meringue, but because it will be broken up into small pieces, it really doesn't matter if you over- or under-bake it. The only tricky thing about this is that the meringue needs to be made the day before you want to eat it.

Serves 4

For the meringue

2 egg whites
½ cup superfine sugar
blue food coloring,
   the gel type

For the filling

1½–2 cups blueberries
2 cups Greek yogurt
edible blue glitter (optional)*

*I say optional, but to
   me it's vital.

Preheat the oven to 275°F and line two baking sheets with parchment paper.

In your OCD-clean bowl, whisk the egg whites good and hard until they're really stiff, so stiff that you could hold the bowl upside down over your head and they wouldn't fall out. Be very sure they are stiff enough before you attempt this maneuver. Add half of the sugar, continuing to whisk until the mixture goes satiny, then add the rest of the sugar.

Using a toothpick, add a small amount of food coloring. Whisk, and. if it's blue enough for you, stop. If you'd prefer it to be more blue,.add a tiny bit more—only a tiny amount, a little goes a long way—and whisk again. When you've achieved the requisite blueness, use a tablespoon to dollop golf ball–sized rounds of meringue onto the baking sheets.

Bake for 1 hour 20 minutes, then turn the oven off and let the meringues sit in there, overnight. (If you need the oven for something else, I'm sure you can take them out and leave them on the countertop. Either way, you must leave them overnight.)

The following day, just before serving, break the meringues up into bite-sized pieces. Place a layer of these blue shards in the bottom of four little bowls. (Use glass bowls for maximum impact, but if you're like me and don't have any glass bowls, you can use wineglasses instead.) Spoon in a layer of blueberries, then a layer of yogurt, then another layer of meringue, and keep going in this fashion until the bowls or glasses are full, then stop. To top everything off, sprinkle with edible blue glitter.

Shirley's Ginger and Pineapple Pavlova

Shirley is my very lovely mother-in-law and effortlessly produces all kinds of baking masterpieces with the minimum of fuss. This is an old favorite of Himself's—he goes misty-eyed whenever he talks about it. I've done my best here, but obviously it can never be as good as the one his mother makes.

Serves 6–8

For the meringue

3 egg whites

¾ cup superfine sugar

For the filling

6 pieces of crystallized ginger

9 ounces fresh pineapple (or canned will do, just drain off the juice from a 16-ounce can)

1 cup heavy cream

1 tablespoon ginger syrup

Preheat the oven to 150°F. Yes, this seems astonishingly low, but the baking goes on for a very long time, between 2½ and 3 hours. Line three baking sheets with parchment paper, then draw one circle on each sheet, 6 inches in diameter. You can draw around the base of a cake pan, or the lid of a saucepan, whatever you have handy.

Whisk the egg whites until they're really stiff. Continuing to whisk, add a spoonful of sugar, then another. Keep at it until all the sugar is in. Divide the mixture equally—or as equally as you can—among the three baking sheets, "filling" the circles. Use your purple spatula (see page 16) to smooth the tops and edges.

Bake for at least 2½ hours, swapping the sheets halfway through the cooking time, until the meringues are hard to the touch and have gone a very pale beige color. If you'd like your cake to have a little bit of chew to it, take it out after 2½ hours, but if you'd prefer it more dry, go for the full 3 hours. Either way, whatever you decide, peel off the parchment paper very carefully—these are fragile—and cool on the baking sheets.

When they're fully cooled, chop the ginger very finely and the pineapple quite finely. Whisk the cream until it's holding its shape but not too stiff, then whip in the ginger syrup. Add the chopped ginger (reserving a sixth for decoration) and pineapple and stir through.

Place one meringue circle on a nice plate and cover it with half of the cream/ginger/pineapple mixture. Place another meringue circle on top of this, then add the rest of the cream. Place—yes! You saw this coming!—your third piece of meringue on top. Neaten it up as best you can and sprinkle the top with the remaining chopped ginger. This is a delicious cake. But not as delicious as if Shirley herself had made it. Obviously.

Zagina Reforma Torta
(Zaga's Reform* Chocolate Cake)

Now, you already know who Zaga is from the honey cake recipe (see page 107) and, like I said, she's an amazing cook.

This is a fabulous cake, very special—Zaga used to make it for Ljiljana's birthdays. It's a meringue that is combined with a high quantity of ground nuts and this makes it quite "cakey," even though there's no flour in it. What is really nice is that the leftover egg yolks are used to create an intensely rich chocolate icing. Usually I don't know what to do with the leftover yolks so I "temporarily" put them in the Bowl of Shame (see page 21). This I put in the fridge, telling myself elaborate lies about all the things I'll make with the yolks—pastry, omelettes, whatever. But I don't and over the next 2 days, the guilt builds and builds until I can hardly go into the kitchen, then at some point I "break," run in really fast and in a mad frenzy, empty the yolks into the bin.

Now, about this cake—it's done in four layers (my first! I'd never gone higher than three layers before!). The multilayeredness is the best thing about it because it's visually stunning, but it means you need four pans (7 inches, if possible). I know most people won't have four pans, all the same size. Maybe you could borrow some? Or you could try baking the bases in two goes? Or, as Zaga says, "One of the ideas is to bake the whole in the big baking sheet that you get with the cooker and then cut it in four pieces."

Serves 12–14

10 eggs

2¼ cups superfine sugar

3 cups hazelnuts, ground to crumbs

5 ounces dark chocolate (70% cocoa solids)

1 cup (2 sticks) butter, at room temperature

*We couldn't get to the bottom of the name. Maybe it's because the eggs get split and then "reform"?

Get a good night's sleep the night before. You need your wits about you for this cake.

Grease four 7-inch pans, then line with parchment paper. Preheat the oven to 350°F.

Separate the eggs. Whisk the 10 egg whites and when they're firm, add 1¼ cups of the sugar, reserving the rest for the icing. Then add the ground hazelnuts, mix well, then pour into your pan (or pans), using your palette knife to smooth the top. Bake for 15 minutes. Turn out onto a wire rack—there might be a bit of a queue—and leave until fully cooled.

Now, for the icing. In a heavy saucepan, bring about 2 quarts of water to a boil. Reduce down to a simmer, then put the bowl containing the 10 egg yolks over the water (but not in it). Add the remaining 1 cup of sugar, then whisk—so that you're heating and whisking simultaneously, if that makes sense. I'd never done this before, it was all new and wonderful.

•••

As the yolks cook, their consistency will change and thicken. We're walking a fine line here because we don't want to scramble the eggs, but they do need to reach 320°F so that they're not raw eggs and so you don't run the risk of giving people—or indeed yourself—salmonella. You can check this by using a thermometer if you have one (I don't). Or else the mixture will coat a metal spoon or bubble at the edge of the bowl. I admit I was very anxious about this, but it was nice to have something real to be anxious about, instead of the usual random free-floating stuff.

When the yolks are hot enough, start dropping the chocolate in, chunk by chunk, so that it melts. Keep whisking. When all the chocolate is melted, take the bowl off the heat and leave to cool fully. Cream the butter and beat it well into the cooled yolky-chocolate mixture.

Then it's time to assemble the cake and this is the bit I found the most challenging. Place a layer of cake on a plate—pick the biggest piece of cake, I know theoretically they're all the same size, but mine weren't—then spread on a thick layer of the icing. Carefully add the next layer of cake (the second biggest) on top of the icing, working hard to center it so that its edges line up with the edges of the layer underneath. This required more skill than I had anticipated.

Spread on another thick layer of icing, then add the next layer of cake and so on until all four layers are stacked (neatly, hopefully) on top of each other, glued together with the lovely thick icing. Cover the top and sides of the cake with the rest of the icing and refrigerate for a couple of hours.

BUT! Watch it like a hawk! Check it every 15 minutes because it might start "sliding"—some of the middle layers might break formation and start bulging like hernias. If this happens, encourage them—gently but firmly—back into place by poking with the flat side of your purple spatula (see page 16). Yes, it happened to me, there was some slippage, but it really didn't matter. People were amazed and astounded by this cake. My friends were in awe and my enemies were sickened.

Banana Meringue Pie

As with the previous recipe, *this* should only be attempted when you have lots of time and a great desire to concentrate on something other than yourself. This is a three-part challenge—you have to make and bake the pastry base (take a look at the Pastry section of this book if you haven't made pastry before), you have to create the banana custard from scratch, and you have to whip, whirl, and bake the meringue topping. Even cutting this beast into slices has to be done in a special way. However! Yes, however! The finished pie looks and tastes AMAZING. You will be so proud of yourself.

Serves 6–8

For the pastry

1⅛ cups all-purpose flour

pinch of salt

7 tablespoons cold butter, cut into cubes

For the banana custard

2 cups milk

½ cup superfine sugar

¾ cup all-purpose flour

¼ teaspoon salt

4 egg yolks (keep the whites for the meringue later)

1 teaspoon banana extract*

4 tablespoons (½ stick) butter, chilled and cut into cubes

4 medium bananas

For the meringue

4 egg whites

¾ cup superfine sugar

¼ teaspoon cream of tartar

pinch of salt

*I know I shouldn't be advocating artificial stuff, but I adore banana extract. I get it in my local Asian shop. It's so riddled with chemicals that I think it might actually be illegal. Nevertheless, delicious.

Make the pastry by sifting the flour and salt into a bowl, then adding the cubed butter. Use the tips of your fingers to rub small pieces of butter and small pieces of flour together, until the mixture begins to resemble fine breadcrumbs. Add a tablespoon or two of cold water if needed.

Refrigerate the pastry for an hour, then roll it out onto a floured surface. Preheat the oven to 350°F, and liberally butter an 8-inch pie plate or dish with a 2-inch depth and line it with the pastry.

Blind bake for 15 minutes, then remove from the oven and keep standing by.

To make the banana custard, start by scalding the milk (see page 21). In a separate saucepan—a big one, big enough to eventually hold all the custard ingredients—sift the sugar, flour, and salt. Gradually whisk in the hot milk. Stirring constantly—the mixture will go really quite thick and resistant, you should build up a bit of a sweat—bring to a boil, cook for 1 minute, then remove from the heat.

In a separate bowl, whisk the egg yolks for a couple of minutes, then slowly add in a cupful of the hot milk/sugar mixture. Keep whisking until fully incorporated, then pour all of this egg yolk/flour/sugar mixture into the saucepan, where the majority of the milk/sugar mixture awaits you. (The reason for all this toing and froing is to even out the temperature, so that the egg yolks don't scramble.)

Cook over low heat for a few minutes and the mixture will thicken up even more. Remove from the heat, then add the banana extract and the cubed butter. Stir until the butter has melted, then leave the mixture to cool down to room temperature. Because this is a custard, there's a high likelihood that a skin will form on the surface. If the thought of this gives you the shudders, cover the custard with a circle of parchment paper—like, literally have the parchment paper resting on the custard, not just above it.

Slice the bananas thinly and line the pastry base with them, in an overlapping pattern. When the custard has cooled, remove the parchment paper. Scoop the custard into the pastry shell, covering the

•••

sliced bananas. Use your purple spatula (see page 16) to spread it evenly. Leave to set for a couple of hours.

When the time is upon you, preheat the oven to 350°F.

Make the meringue by beating the egg whites until they're stiff. Gradually add the sugar, then the cream of tartar and salt. Swirl the meringue on top of the set custard, making sure it comes right to the edges of the pastry because when it bakes and eventually cools, it will contract slightly and you don't want it exposing the filling underneath.

Bake for 20 minutes, until it's a pale beige color and crisp to the touch. However! WARNING! WARNING! WARNING! The eggs won't be cooked through, so don't give this otherwise impeccable pie to vulnerable types—by that, I mean children, old folk, pregnant women, and people with compromised immune systems. It's very unlikely that they'll get salmonella, but like I said on page 108, we live in litigious times. Also, you don't want anything bad on your conscience—God knows, we struggle enough with existential guilt without having poisoned someone, no? Cool the pie on a rack, then refrigerate for a couple of hours.

To slice: SPECIAL INSTRUCTIONS! Have a bowl of very hot water standing by. Dip a sharp knife into the hot water, and cut a slice through the meringue, but not down into the custard and pastry. Dip the knife into the water again, then do another slice through the meringue. Continue to mark out slices through the meringue, re-dipping the knife in the water after each go. When all the slices are marked out in the meringue, then, and only then, cut all the way down through the custard and pastry. Serve cold.

You can do this; you CAN make **MACARONS**. However, they will not be all lovely and neat and the same size, the way they are in Ladurée. Can you make your peace with that? If not, stop right here, you'll only wreck your head. But if you can accept that your macarons may be bockety and funny-shaped and still worthy of existence, then proceed.

To get the same consistency every time, professional bakers weigh their egg whites, allowing only a certain amount into the bowl. However, we are not professional bakers. We take our chances, we live on the edge, we accept that some egg whites are bigger than others and therefore every batch of macarons we make will be unique. We do not despair over this, oh no, we celebrate their individuality.

COOKIES

Orange and Fennel Tuiles

Chocolate and Treacle Cookies

Breakfast Bars

Shakar Loqum (Armenian Sugar Cookies)

Lebkuchen Hearts

Pistachio Biscotti

Defibrillator Cubes

Luxury Blueberry, Pine Nut, and Chocolate Cookies

Shoe and Handbag Cookies

There's such a massive universe of **COOKIES** out there for our delectation that at times it really does make me believe in a benign God. Never mind butterflies; never mind a newborn baby's foot. For me it's all about the cookies! God created a world where cookies exist! When you look at it like that, how could She be anything but a decent sort!

Obviously, you'd need to write an entire encyclopedia to cover the multitude of cookies in the world and all I have available is a chapter. So I've made a pitiful attempt (the nerve of me, the neck of me, the grandiosity of me) to give the merest glimpse of what's available to us. I've started with thin and sophisticated tuiles, made my way to rustic oaty bruisers, and done some detours en route.

I must admit to you that of all the things I've ever baked, making cookies has given me the most pleasure. Because it's where I get to use my (many, many) cookie cutters and really, I cannot tell you! I get to make shoes. Edible shoes. And handbags. And owls. And stars. And hearts. If I found out I had an hour left to live, I'd use the time to make shoe cookies. Fact.

Orange and Fennel Tuiles

These are very much "lady" biscuits. Like, you wouldn't serve them to the man who's come to fix your washing machine. Not unless you wanted him to stalk out in disgust. Nevertheless, in their thin, delicate, melt-in-the-mouth way, these are fabulous—sort of like orange-and-fennel-flavored air.

One important thing to note, though, is that it seems to be the "done thing" to "shape" one's tuiles so that they're curved. From what I can gather, flatness in a tuile is not considered to be a good look.

The best way to curve them is, *the very second* they come out of the oven, to lay them on a rolling pin or wine bottle and press gently. They'll take on the shape of the pin or bottle but won't break. However, please be aware that they're pliable only for *a very short time*. I mean, literally seconds. Perhaps 30. I've discovered the hard way that the best way to do this is to remove maybe three or four tuiles from the oven, lay them on whatever curved thing you're using, let them cool, move them onto a plate, then take three or four more tuiles out of the oven and start again. The good thing is that they cool and set really quickly, so at least you won't have to do too much hanging around.

Makes approx. 15

3½ tablespoons butter
½ teaspoon fennel seeds
2 egg whites
1 cup confectioners' sugar
½ cup all-purpose flour
zest of 1 orange

Line two large baking sheets with parchment paper and preheat your oven to 350°F.

Melt the butter and set aside until fully cooled.

Grind the fennel seeds well to release their flavor.

Whip the egg whites until they hold soft peaks.

Sift in the confectioners' sugar and flour, then add the orange zest, fennel seeds, and the melted, cooled butter. Fold through with as light a touch as you can manage.

For each tuile, pour a level soup spoon of the mix, which will be quite runny, onto the parchment paper and leave room—a good 1 inch between each—for spreading. Keep going until you've used up all the mixture. The tuiles will look very insubstantial, almost see-through. Don't worry, they're meant to.

Bake for between 6 and 12 minutes, until the tuiles are golden around the edges but still pale in the middle. Use your palette knife to gently remove them from the parchment paper. If you're planning on "shaping" them, now's your time.

Serve to people who don't really believe in eating.

Chocolate and Treacle Cookies

Dark, rich, sophisticated chocolate cookies. The treacle (molasses may be substituted) adds an extra depth of flavor.

5 ounces dark chocolate
  (70% cocoa solids)

7 tablespoons butter

¾ cup light brown sugar

1 egg

1 tablespoon black treacle
  (or molasses)

1 cup all-purpose flour

⅓ cup cocoa powder

pinch of salt

Line two big baking sheets with parchment paper.

Melt the chocolate using your preferred method (see page 20) and let it cool for 10 to 15 minutes.

Then—and only then—preheat the oven to 350°F.

Beat the butter and sugar until pale and fluffy.

Add in the egg and treacle and mix well.

Add the (cooled) melted chocolate and keep mixing.

Sift in the flour, the cocoa powder, and the pinch of salt and fold through.

Using two soup spoons, scoop up golf ball–sized lumps of the dough (it will be very sticky) and place on the parchment paper.

Keep plenty of space between them—they will spread.

Bake for 15 minutes, but check on them after about 12 because these have a tendency to burn.

Cool the sheets on wire racks. The cookies will still be quite soft at this stage so don't be "at" them. After perhaps half an hour, gently remove them from their sheets, but keep them cooling on the racks. After a while the outsides of the cookies will crisp up and the insides will be wonderfully melty and chocolatey.

Breakfast Bars

This almost qualifies as healthy eating. I started making these when myself and a group of friends decided we needed a hobby and fixed on hill walking in Wicklow. The nuts, seeds, and dried fruit give me the energy to go for the final push when I'm trudging up the side of a mountain, and the condensed milk gives a bit of sweet comfort when the sleet is blowing in my face, I feel like crying, and I wish I'd picked a different hobby, maybe doing stained glass.

Makes 14

¾ cup sweetened condensed milk

1 cup rolled oats

¾ cup dried apricots

2 ounces crystallized ginger

1 cup hazelnuts

½ cup pumpkin seeds

¼ cup sunflower seeds

1 tablespoon cocoa powder (optional)*

*In fact, it's so optional that it doesn't exist on my official list of ingredients. I prefer to lie about its presence because people feel so virtuous eating these delicious bars that I'd feel bad about wrecking their buzz.

Preheat the oven to 250°F. Line an 8-inch square pan with parchment paper.

Gently heat the condensed milk in a saucepan.

Put the rolled oats in a separate bowl.

Chop the apricots and ginger and halve the hazelnuts, then add to the oats, along with the pumpkin and sunflower seeds.

Pour in the condensed milk and stir well. The mixture will go lovely and sticky.

Add the sneaky tablespoon of cocoa powder, then wipe the whole episode from your mind.

Pile the mixture into the pan and pack down well, getting into all the corners. Flatten the surface using the back of a tablespoon dipped in water.

Bake for an hour.

Cool on a wire rack, then remove from the pan and cut into bar shapes, roughly 4 inches by 1¼ inches.

Climb the side of a hill, then eat without guilt.

Shakar Loqum (Armenian Sugar Cookies)

This is an amazing recipe from my brother-in-law, Sean, who is an absolute genius in the kitchen. His mother, JoAnn, was of Armenian descent and Sean sent me this recipe, entitled, "From my mom's recipe box." I found this almost unbearably poignant, as JoAnn died way too young. But maybe it's of some comfort to know that so many of us are enjoying the sugar cookies she used to make.

These diamond-shaped cookies are intense—buttery, sweet, and slightly crumbly. Don't be alarmed by how small they are—they are so very, very rich that to make them any bigger would lessen their impact. Also, they might trigger a cardiac arrest.

Makes about 22 cookies

12 ounces clarified butter—
    also known as ghee*

¾ cup superfine sugar

pinch of salt

pinch of baking powder

2 eggs, separated

3 cups all-purpose flour

approximately 30 slivered
    almonds

*You can get clarified butter in Indian shops. Or you can make your own, but it's pretty labor intensive. Also, I find the idea of doing it terribly frightening, but you might not. Here are JoAnn's instructions:

Melt about 2 cups (4 sticks) butter over low heat until foam appears. Skim off the foam using a knife and keep on the low heat for about 15 minutes. During this time, water will evaporate and salts and solids will settle at the bottom of the pan. Cool for about 15 to 20 minutes, then carefully pour the clarified butter into a container, leaving the salts and solids at the bottom of the pan. You can discard these.

Grease and line an 8-inch loose-bottomed square pan and preheat the oven to 350°F.

Whisk the clarified butter, then add the sugar, salt, and baking powder and mix well. Add the egg yolks and mix again. Sift in the flour, stir it through with a wooden spoon, then use your hands to shape the dough. Press the dough into the prepared pan and flatten it with the base of a glass.

Now, things get a little tricky. The authentic way to make Shakar Loqum is to cut the uncooked dough into diamond shapes, and it was the part of the recipe I found most challenging. You might find it helpful (I did) to do a dry run first by getting a sheet of paper, the same size as the baking pan, and draw the diamond patterns, so that you know what you want to re-create with the dough. (To be quite honest, I got Himself to do it. He's good that way, patient and mathematical.)

Draw diagonal lines, approximately 1 inch apart, going in one direction, then draw diagonal lines going in the opposite direction, also about 1 inch apart. Remember that you want diamond shapes, not squares, so the lines should be at a fairly acute angle. You want long, narrow cookies, not short, squat ones. Am I making any sense to you at all? If not, I'm so sorry. Just look at the picture if you're confused.

Now re-create your drawing by using a small sharp knife to cut the uncooked dough into diamond shapes, the same size and shape as the ones in your drawing. You can now discard your piece of paper.

Place a slice of almond into the middle of each diamond shape. Beat the egg whites lightly, then brush the top of the dough with them. (You won't get to use all the egg whites.)

Bake for 15 minutes, then reduce the oven heat to 300°F and bake for about another 20 minutes, until the cookies are a golden brown color.

Remove the pan from the oven and while the cookies are still warm (and still in the pan), recut the diamond shapes—by that I mean go

•••

over the pre-existing "cuts" with the same small sharp knife, so that the cookies will fully separate into diamond shapes when they're eventually removed from the pan. It may not be immediately obvious where the diagonal lines are, but actually the almond slivers work as great reference points.

Wait until they're fully cooled before carefully removing the cookies from the pan.

There will be a few leftover bits of cookie at the sides of the pan that didn't make it into the diamond shapes. This might initially strike you as wastage, but then remind yourself of what Confucius once said (at least I think it was him). "Broken Cookies Don't Count." Eat them without guilt.

Thanks, JoAnn. (And thanks, Sean.)

Lebkuchen Hearts

The first time I encountered these delicious spicy German cookies was one Christmas several years ago when my German publisher sent me a massive one (about 8 inches in diameter) with *Ich Liebe Dich* iced on it (which means "I Love You"). I was thrilled and all set to tuck into it until Himself suggested that the fact it was hanging off a ribbon meant that it was probably intended to be a Christmas decoration, rather than a Christmas sweetmeat. This, of course, came as a terrible disappointment to me.

So I investigated the whole Lebkuchen Hearts business and discovered that yes, there is a German tradition of giving them as home decorations. Or sometimes the recipient wears them on a ribbon around their neck (I think that's *gorgeous.*) And it seems to be the done thing to ice cute sayings on them.

But the point I'm trying to make is that these cookies *can* be eaten. In fact, they *should* be eaten because they taste fabulous.

Don't be alarmed by the long list of spices in the recipe. I think the most important one is ginger and if you don't have any of the others, don't fret.

Finally, as these are Lebkuchen *Hearts*, you'll need some sort of heart-shaped cookie cutter. If you don't have any, you could try freestyling with a sharp knife. Or you could simply use a different-shaped cutter and change the name of the cookies to—oh, just off the top of my head— Lebkuchen Shoes. Or Lebkuchen Handbags.

•••

Makes approximately
 18 heart-shaped cookies
 (4 inches at their widest
 point) or 3 giant ones
 (10 inches at their widest
 point)

7 tablespoons butter

¾ cup honey

½ cup light brown sugar

1 teaspoon ground ginger

1 teaspoon ground coriander

1 teaspoon ground cinnamon

1 teaspoon ground allspice

½ teaspoon ground nutmeg

2 cloves, bashed

1 star anise

6 cardamom pods, bashed

2½ tablespoons cocoa
 powder

5 cups all-purpose flour

pinch of salt

1½ teaspoons baking powder

1 egg

To decorate

writing icing

If you want to keep things
authentically German, here
are a few handy phrases:

Ich liebe dich
 (I love you)

Ich liebe schuhe
 (I love shoes)

Fröhliche Weihnachten
 (Happy Christmas)

Place the butter, honey, sugar, spices, and cocoa powder in a medium-sized saucepan and heat gently. Stir until the sugar dissolves and the whole mixture looks dark and treacly. Be careful not to let it burn. Take off the heat and cool slightly, and remove the cardamom, star anise, and cloves.

Sift the flour with the salt and baking powder into a bowl. Using your fist, make a crater in the flour and add the egg, then pour in the honey mixture. Mix on a low speed and eventually a ball of dough will form.

Divide it roughly into two, wrap each lump in plastic wrap, and stick in the fridge for at least a couple of hours (you could leave it as long as a couple of days).

When you're ready to make your hearts, line two baking sheets with parchment paper and heat the oven to 350°F.

Scatter your work surface with flour and roll out one of your lumps of dough until it's about ½ inch thick. These are quite hefty creatures, so no need to roll them out too thin.

If you're going for the 4-inch heart-shaped cookies, press the cutter right down into the rolled-out dough until it reaches the floured surface, then give it a tiny little "shimmy" to loosen it. Gently maneuver your palette knife under the raw cookie and lift onto the baking sheet. If it all goes a bit gammy, and it might well, especially if you're new to this game, just roll out the dough and try again. (The experts say you shouldn't roll out dough more than once, that it makes it slightly tough, but it's all very well for them, after all, they're *experts*.)

Remember if you want to make hearts that will hang from a ribbon, create a little hole for the ribbon to go through.

To make a giant heart, as I say, you can freestyle or if you're lucky enough (as I am) to have a heart-shaped pan, press it down onto the dough and cut around it. That bit went okay. It was when I tried to transfer the heart onto the baking sheet that it went awry on me and broke in half (metaphor, inadvertent, but clearly no escaping it). However, I pieced it back together and although you could still see the seam, it was grand. (Another metaphor, obviously.)

Roll out your second lump of dough and repeat the process.

Bake for 15 to 20 minutes, watching that they don't burn on the bottom. Obviously the bigger the cookie, the longer it will take.

Let the cookies cool completely on their sheet. They will harden as they cool.

You can serve these plain—they are really delicious, dark and spicy, and very Christmassy. Or you can decorate with writing icing.

Pistachio Biscotti

Homemade biscotti! The thrill! Who knew such things were possible? This recipe calls for a tablespoon of nut oil and I've suggested using pistachio oil because once upon a time, by bizarre chance, I found a can of it (not even a jar! A can!) gathering dust at the back of a shelf in a faraway deli and have been looking for a chance to use it ever since. I'd never seen such a thing as pistachio oil before, or since, and the likelihood of you being able to lay your hands on some might be slim. In which case, use olive oil instead and don't give it a moment's worry.

Makes 12–14 biscotti

1 cup all-purpose flour

½ teaspoon baking powder

1 tablespoon cocoa powder

⅓ cup superfine sugar

2 tablespoons butter, chilled
  and cut into cubes

1 egg

1 tablespoon pistachio oil*

¼ cup pistachios, halved

2 ounces dark chocolate
  (70% cocoa solids),
  chopped roughly

*Or if, as it almost certainly will, it proves impossible to find, olive oil will do instead.

Line a baking sheet with wax paper and preheat the oven to 325°F.

Sift the flour, baking powder, and cocoa powder into a bowl, then stir in the sugar.

Add the butter and either rub in with your fingertips or blitz with your machine until the butter has all "disappeared." The mixture will look like dark sand.

Beat the egg and the oil together, then add to the flour/cocoa, etc. and mix well. At this stage it should start coming together to form a dough.

Add the pistachios and chopped chocolate and stir to distribute evenly.

Sprinkle your countertop with flour. Divide the dough into two and, using your hands, roll it out into two logs, each about 10 inches long. Slightly flatten the logs until they are 1½ to 2 inches wide.

Bake for 20 minutes. Remove from the oven and lower the temperature to 300°F.

Using a serrated knife, slice each log into six or seven evenly sized pieces. Gently, because at this stage they're soft and fragile, put some space between each biscotto (singular of biscotti, I'm guessing!), then return to the oven for 10 minutes to dry out.

Remove from the oven and leave in the air to firm up and harden for a couple of hours.

Defibrillator Cubes

So called because these peanut, honey, and banana squares are so tightly packed full of dense energy they could probably bring a person back from the dead. They're similar to the Breakfast Bars on page 164 in that they're both oat-based, but these are the turbo-charged versions.

Makes 16 squares

½ cup (1 stick) butter

½ cup crunchy peanut butter

¾ cup light brown sugar

¼ cup honey

1 cup rolled oats

3½ ounces dried bananas, chopped finely

⅓ cup roasted salted peanuts

Grease and line an 8-inch square pan. Preheat the oven to 325°F.

Put the butter, peanut butter, sugar, and honey into a BIG saucepan (big enough to eventually fit the rolled oats and other ingredients). Gently heat until all the butters melt and the sugar dissolves.

Stir in the rolled oats, chopped dried banana, and peanuts and distribute evenly.

Pour into the prepared pan, getting the mixture into all the corners. Flatten with the back of a wet tablespoon and bake for 30 minutes.

Cool on a baking sheet and leave for a long time, preferably overnight, before removing from the pan and cutting into squares. They will be sticky, caramelly, and utterly delicious, and don't be worried that they might look small because, believe me, a little goes a long, long way.

Luxury Blueberry, Pine Nut, and Chocolate Cookies

I have a tendency to overdo everything and these yummy cookies are packed tight with "stuff"—blueberries, pine nuts, and chocolate chips. If you'd prefer your ratio of cookie dough to "bits" to be a little less decadent, then just reduce the amount of berries, nuts, and chocolate chips you add. In fact, you can reduce the quantities by half and you'll still get fabulous cookies. Also, bear in mind, you can add any version of dried fruit and nuts. But try to make sure they're "harmonious"—what I mean is that, for example, here, the sourness of the blueberries goes very well with the slight bitterness of the dark chocolate. And my one other tip is that whatever fruits and nuts you add, try to make sure that they're roughly the same size—in these cookies, the blueberries are roughly the same size as the pine nuts. What you don't want is *imbalance.*

These cookies include rolled oats, so they have a slightly rustic texture. But they taste so great that they'd be good enough to serve should anyone important ever be visiting you. Like, if George Michael just happened to drop in. (God, how I wish . . .)

Makes approximately 18–20 cookies

½ cup (1 stick) butter
½ cup light brown sugar
⅛ cup dark brown sugar
1 egg
1 cup all-purpose flour
⅓ cup cocoa powder
pinch of salt
½ teaspoon baking powder
½ cup rolled oats
3½ ounces dried blueberries
¾ cup pine nuts
½ cup dark chocolate chips (70% cocoa solids)

Line two large baking sheets with parchment paper. Preheat the oven to 350°F.

Beat the butter and sugars well together. Add the egg and beat again.

Sift in the flour, cocoa powder, salt, and baking powder and fold through.

Stir in the oats, blueberries, pine nuts, and chocolate chips, distributing them evenly throughout. You might want to add the berries, nuts, and chocolate chips in batches, so that if at some stage you feel the mixture looks full enough, you can stop.

Using a soup spoon, scoop up rounds of the dough, roughly about the size of a golf ball, and use your hands to roll into a fairly flattened ball shape—your hands will get good and sticky but what harm—then place on the baking sheet.

Leave plenty of space between each cookie because they'll spread as they cook.

Bake for 15 minutes, then cool the tray on a wire rack. Don't interfere with the cookies until they're fully cooled because they'll be soft.

Then they'll be absolutely delicious—crunchy on the outside and melty and wonderful on the inside and—of course—jam-packed with bits and pieces.

Shoe and Handbag Cookies

You don't only have to make shoe and handbag cookies with this recipe. You can make *anything*. Anything! Your only limitation is your imagination. Also, the cookie cutters you have.

The flavoring I've used here is plain vanilla, but you can substitute any number of things—a teaspoon of dried cinnamon, the zest of half a lemon, or a splash of Cointreau. For example, I've made cardamom and rosewater cookies by adding four ground cardamom pods and a teaspoon of rosewater instead of the vanilla. I've also made lime and ginger cookies by leaving out the vanilla and adding a teaspoon each of dried ginger and lime zest. It's up to you. Have fun. Go mad.

The same with the decorating. I've given you a basic glacé icing recipe, but you can dye it countless different colors and use writing icing, glitter, edible stars, sugar balls, and so on to create any number of effects. There are plenty of websites that specialize in edible cake decorations and you will be introduced to a veritable wonderland. But a word of warning—once you start, you can't stop. You'll find yourself thinking, but I simply MUST have some of these tiny sugar cats! How can I make cookies and hold my head up in polite society if they're not sprinkled with tiny sugar cats? Or mini candy canes! Or miniature edible butterflies!

If you're in any way prone to addiction, you could be in choppy waters here.

Makes a variable number depending on the size and shape of your cutters!

For the biscuits

1¾ sticks butter, at room temperature

1 cup superfine sugar

1 vanilla pod

1 egg, beaten

3¼ cups all-purpose flour

For the icing

4 cups confectioners' sugar

your choice of icing color, writing icing, and edible decorations

Beat the butter and sugar together until light and fluffy.

Scrape the vanilla seeds from the pod and add to the mixture. Discard the pod.

Beat in the egg and sift in the flour. Mix until a soft dough forms.

Divide the dough into two roughly equal-sized balls, cover with plastic wrap, and refrigerate for at least an hour.

Line three baking sheets with parchment paper. Preheat the oven to 350°F.

Take the balls of pastry out of the fridge, remove the plastic wrap, and divide each one into two.

Roll one of the lumps out on a well-floured surface to a thickness of about ⅛ inch. This is something you'll get better at gauging the more you do it, but there are some tools you can get in the specialized baking shops, such as special rubber bands to put on both ends of your rolling pin that limit the thickness of whatever you're rolling out, or "guide sticks"—pieces of wood ⅛ inch thick—that you place on either side of the pastry so you don't roll anything thinner. •••

Use the cookie cutter of your choice to cut out shapes. Press the cutter right down until it reaches the floured surface, then give it a tiny little "shimmy" to loosen the shape from the pastry around it. Gently maneuver your palette knife under it and lift onto the parchment paper. If it all goes a bit wrong, and it might well, especially if you're a beginner, then just roll out the pastry and try again.

You only need to leave about a half inch between each cookie on the sheet because they don't spread much.

Gather up the scraps of unused pastry, roll them into your next ball of pastry, and repeat until all your pastry is in cookie shapes.

Bake for 9 to 12 minutes, until the cookies are a—funny, this—*cookie* color and are set but not too hard.

Take the sheets from the oven and use your palette knife to lift each cookie onto a wire rack. Cool.

Now for the icing. Use a wide-bottomed shallow bowl (that's assuming you have one and if you don't, don't worry, any bowl will do). Mix the confectioners' sugar with 4 tablespoons cold water and your desired coloring until you have the runniness you desire.

Place a cookie, facedown, in the bowl of icing until one surface is entirely covered. Tilt it from side to side, letting the excess icing run off (this is a messy business), then place on a wire rack. Even more icing might run off then. All fine. (You could place paper towels under the trays if you're worried about the mess.) Do a batch of perhaps eight cookies, then decorate them before the icing has the chance to set. I use writing icing to define the edges and give a more "finished" look, but that's entirely up to you. Either way, I predict you'll have a wonderful, wonderful, wonderful time. You'll feel like a child again.

FRUIT AND VEG

Beet Cake

Orange and Cashew Cake

Sweet Potato Pie

Chocolate Squash Bake

Tamarind, Date, and Sour Cherry Muffins

Mango Upside-Down Cake

Raspberry and Strawberry Upside-Down Cake

Pear, Almond, and Tahini Cake

German Stollen Cake

Corn, Coconut, and Lime Loaf

The healthy section!
A great way to get
your 5 a day. Er . . . yes.

Beet Cake

When I was young, I couldn't imagine anything more horrible than beets. I mean, *beets*. It was a strange, disgusting red ball that my father used to have with his salad and I was so horrified by it that whenever the jar appeared, I had to leave the house. Now I am older and less extreme in my opinions, I have tasted the fruit of the beetroot tree and I know it to be delicious.

Nevertheless, a funny choice for a cake, no? Well, no. Not when you think of carrot cake. After all, that's a root vegetable that has been successfully turned into cake. So why not beets? Well, when you put it like that . . .

It was hard though, hard to stop thinking of beets as a dinner ingredient and to start thinking of them as something that could coexist with sugar. I had to expend a lot of energy in a radical recalibration of my mental sweet/savory interface. So much so that I couldn't summon the requisite will to grate raw beets. Yes, I decided to take the easy option and use beets that were already cooked. I urge you to do the same—raw beets are the hardest substance known to man. Also the reddest. It would take a day and a half to grate enough raw beets for this cake and your entire street would be dyed vermilion forever.

Makes about 12 slices

For the cake

9 ounces cooked beets
(not in vinegar or brine or anything)
3½ ounces dark chocolate
(70% cocoa solids)
½ cup (1 stick) butter
¾ cup dark brown sugar
¾ cup light brown sugar
3 eggs, beaten
1¾ cups self-rising flour
⅓ cup cocoa powder
pinch of salt

To decorate

¾ cup confectioners' sugar
red gel food coloring*
box of Nerds candy

Preheat the oven to 350°F and grease and line a 9-inch cake pan. Grate the beets and set aside.

Melt the chocolate using your favored method (see page 20) and set that aside too. Cream the butter and sugars and gradually add the eggs. Sift the flour, cocoa powder, and salt into the butter mixture.

Stir in the beets, then the melted chocolate. Scrape the mixture into the prepared pan and bake for 35 to 50 minutes. Do the Skewer Test (see page 23) and when you're happy, put the pan on a wire rack. When the cake is cool, take it out of the pan.

Make the icing by adding 1 tablespoon water to the confectioners' sugar. If it's too thick, add a *little* more water, but go easy, you don't want it too runny. Add the red food coloring. Pour it over the top of the cake and let it run down the sides. Finally, scatter the Nerds.

Orange and Cashew Cake

This is a fine, hefty cake, quite massive, and should feed several hundred people. I was slightly worried that the bread crumbs might weight it down, but the egg whites counterbalance any possible heaviness and the addition of the orange syrup is a delightful, citrusy game changer.

Makes at least 20 slices

½ cup (1 stick) butter

¾ cup superfine sugar

3 eggs, separated

¾ cup ground cashews

¾ cup bread crumbs

½ cup orange juice

1 teaspoon grated orange zest

2½ cups all-purpose flour

1 tablespoon baking powder

For the orange syrup

¾ cup superfine sugar

¼ cup orange juice

Preheat the oven to 350°F and liberally (wonderful word!) grease a 10-inch Bundt pan.

Cream together the butter, sugar, and egg yolks. Add the ground cashews, bread crumbs, orange juice, and orange zest. Sift in the flour and baking powder and fold through. In a separate bowl, beat the egg whites until stiff, then fold gently into the mixture.

Spoon the mixture into the pan and bake for approximately 55 minutes, until the outside has gone lovely and crusty. Remove from the oven and put on a wire rack, but don't take the cake out of the pan! It needs to stay *in situ* until it absorbs the orange syrup.

Meanwhile, make the syrup by heating the sugar and orange juice gently. Stir until the sugar has dissolved. Prick the surface of the cake with a fork—lots and lots of times, but gently, you want to puncture, not fracture—then pour over the syrup and leave to infuse for as long as possible; overnight would be wonderful. Cut into slices and serve to multitudes (in reality, it makes about 20 slices).

Sweet Potato Pie

Exotic as this pie is, it's actually very simple to make. And you can make it super-simple if you use a store-bought, pre-baked pastry shell, but it must be at least 1¼ inches deep to fit all the filling. If you decide to make your own pastry shell and you're new to pastry, take a look at the Pastry section of this book (see page 112) before you go any further.

Serves 8

For the pastry

1⅓ cups all-purpose flour

pinch of salt

7 tablespoons cold butter, cut into cubes

OR

1 8-inch pre-baked shortcrust pastry shell, at least 1¼ inches deep

For the pie

1⅓ pounds sweet potatoes, peeled and cut into cubes

2 eggs

⅓ cup light brown sugar

3 tablespoons maple syrup

½ teaspoon ground cinnamon

½ teaspoon ground nutmeg

1 scant cup heavy double cream

To serve

store-bought chocolate sauce in a squeezy bottle

If you're making your own pastry, sift the flour and salt into a bowl, then add the cubed butter. Use the tips of your fingers to rub small pieces of butter and small pieces of flour together, until the mixture begins to resemble fine bread crumbs. Add a tablespoon or two of cold water if needed.

Refrigerate the pastry for an hour, then roll it out onto a floured surface. Preheat the oven to 350°F, then liberally butter an 8-inch pie plate with a 1¼-inch depth, and line it with the pastry.

Blind bake for 15 minutes, then remove from the oven and keep standing by.

In a large saucepan of water, bring the sweet potato cubes to a boil, then reduce to a simmer for about 15 minutes, until soft. Drain, then puree. You can do this by mashing or by using a food processor, but make sure it's *completely* smooth, with no dodgy lumps still hanging around. Leave to cool fully.

Preheat the oven to 375°F. Put the pastry shell on a baking sheet.

Whisk the eggs, sugar, and maple syrup, then add the pureed sweet potato, the cinnamon, nutmeg, and cream. Pour into the pastry shell.

Bake for approximately 40 to 50 minutes, until almost set, but still with a slight wobble in the center. Keep an eye on the pastry because as it's already baked, there's a chance the edges might burn. If they look like they might be going too dark, cover loosely with aluminum foil.

Cool on a wire rack, then chill in the fridge for at least an hour. Just before serving, drizzle with the store-bought chocolate sauce.

Chocolate Squash Bake

Again, as with the Beet Cake, I beg of you to keep an open mind here. Certainly for me, the notion of using squash in a sweet cake was a challenging one, but my reservations lasted just as long as it took me to eat a slice. This really works, especially with the addition of the figs, which give a lovely sticky texture.

I've used a big baking sheet so that the cake comes out quite shallow and flat. Don't be alarmed by this—it is dense and muscular enough to hold its own.

It would be perfectly acceptable to serve this cake plain and unadorned, but I've covered mine with a layer of chocolate ganache because I have difficulty with the concept of restraint.

Makes 21 fingers

3½ ounces squash, such as butternut

8 ounces dark chocolate (70% cocoa solids)

¾ cup (1½ sticks) butter

3 eggs

1 cup dark brown sugar

½ cup light brown sugar

2 cups all-purpose flour

1 tablespoon baking powder

5 ounces dried figs, chopped small

For the ganache

7 ounces dark chocolate (70% cocoa solids)

½ cup heavy cream

colored chocolate vermicelli sprinkies

Preheat the oven to 350°F. Grease and line a 12-inch-by-9-inch baking sheet. Grate the squash and set aside.

Melt the chocolate and butter together in a heatproof bowl over a saucepan of hot water. In a separate bowl, beat the eggs with the sugars, then add the melted chocolate and butter. Stir in 1 cup cold water, then sift in the flour and baking powder. Add the grated squash and chopped figs and mix well.

Pour into the prepared sheet and bake for approximately 50 minutes. Do the Skewer Test (see page 23), then cool on a wire rack.

When the cake is fully cooled, prepare the chocolate ganache by melting the chocolate using your favored method (see page 20) and stirring in the cream. Pour over the cake and scatter with chocolate vermicelli sprinkles.

When this is set, it's time to cut the cake into fingers, each approximately 4 inches by 1 inch. Because this is such a big cake—"unwieldy" you could say—it might be easier to do the cutting while the cake is still in the sheet.

Tamarind, Date, and Sour Cherry Muffins

Tamarind is my "thing," the ingredient that I bandy around in conversations when I want to sound like I'm an adventurous and pioneering baker. "Oh yes," I say, striving to sound casual, "I find that a teaspoon of tamarind gives a wonderfully intriguing sourness." And then I say a little prayer and hope I get the chance to make a face of mock surprise and say, "You don't know what tamarind is?! Well, I believe it's some sort of fruit, originally from Sudan, used a lot in Malaysian cooking, or so I'm told."

Anyway, tamarind isn't half as exotic as it used to be. Time was you had to go to the Asian market—or indeed Malaysia itself—to get tamarind paste, but now it can be bought in my local supermarket.

The one thing about tamarind that remains as true as when I first began baking with it is that it really *does* give a wonderfully intriguing sourness—so sour, in fact, that I would strongly urge caution when it comes to licking the spoon after you've been dealing with it.

However, it works really well in this recipe. Itself and the cherries lead a spirited crusade of sourness, which is brought to heel by the powerful dark forces of the dates and the brown sugar. (Sorry about that sentence, I've been watching *Camelot*.)

Now, about "muffins." I'm not sure at what size cupcakes stop being cupcakes and officially become large enough to be called "muffins." I'm calling these little cakes "muffins," but I'm worried about misleading you. As muffins go, they're probably at the smaller end of the scale, so if you'd prefer to call them "cupcakes," then work away. I've decorated them with a simple glacé icing, colored orange.

Makes 12

3½ ounces dried dates

3½ ounces dried sour cherries

½ cup (1 stick) butter

1 ounce tamarind paste

2 eggs

⅓ cup dark brown sugar

1 cup all-purpose flour

1 teaspoon baking soda

For the icing

¼ cup confectioners' sugar

4 tablespoons water or lime juice

orange food coloring

1 ounce dried sour cherries

Preheat the oven to 350°F and line a 12-hole muffin (or cupcake) pan with paper liners.

Chop the dates and sour cherries very finely, then place in a saucepan with ⅔ cup water and bring to a boil. Boil for 1 minute, then remove from the heat and add the butter. Stir until it has melted, then add the tamarind and leave to cool for maybe 10 minutes.

In a separate bowl, whisk the eggs and sugar. Add the cooled fruit/butter mixture, then sift in the flour and baking soda and fold through. Don't worry if the sugar goes hard and lumpy, the lumps will dissolve during the baking time. Divide the mixture among the paper liners and bake for about 15 to 17 minutes. Cool the pan on a wire rack.

Make the icing by gradually adding the water or lime juice to the confectioners' sugar, until you've achieved your desired runniness. Then add the orange food coloring. Spoon the icing over the top of each muffin and use a knife to encourage it to the edges. Scatter the chopped cherries in a little heap in the center. Practice saying the words, "wonderfully intriguing sourness" in front of the mirror, then serve.

Mango Upside-Down Cake

A variation of the childhood favorite, Pineapple Upside-Down Cake. It is phenomenally easy to make.

Serves 6–8

For the topping

3½ tablespoons butter

¼ cup light brown sugar

16-ounce can of sliced mango in syrup, drained (Reserve 2 tablespoons of the syrup.)

For the cake

7 tablespoons butter

¼ cup superfine sugar

2 eggs

¾ cup self-rising flour

1 teaspoon baking powder

Liberally grease an 8-inch cake pan. This is actually one situation where I would counsel *against* using a loose-bottomed or springform pan because the first time I made this cake, I had "leakage." The juice from the mango made its way out through the gap in my pan and covered the base of the oven with a—frankly delicious—sort of caramel. Preheat the oven to 350°F.

For the topping, beat the butter and sugar together, then spread it over the base of the cake pan—it will be a very thin layer, do not be alarmed. Then arrange the drained mango slices on top of the topping, in the most artistic way you can manage. Feel free to cut the slices up to plug any gaps.

Make the cake by creaming the butter and sugar together, adding the eggs and the 2 tablespoons of reserved mango syrup. Sift in the flour and baking powder and fold through.

Spread the cake batter over the sliced mangoes, covering them, then bake for 35 minutes. Cool for 5 minutes—yes, only 5 minutes—on a wire rack then, trying not to burn your fingers, turn the cake out onto a serving plate. Serve warm, with a dollop of fresh cream.

Raspberry and Strawberry Upside-Down Cake

In a way, you might think I have a bit of a cheek, fobbing you off with this recipe, which is very, very similar to the Mango Upside-Down Cake I've just given you. But even though the cake part is—yes, I admit it—*identical*, the fruit is so different that this is an entirely different cake. Also, I've baked this cake in a heart-shaped pan and because the fruit here is red, it looks fantastic.

Serves 6–8

For the topping

3½ tablespoons butter

¼ cup light brown sugar

15-ounce can of raspberries in juice, drained

15-ounce can of strawberries in juice, drained

(Reserve 2 tablespoons of the juice.)

For the cake

7 tablespoons butter

½ cup superfine sugar

¾ cup self-rising flour

2 eggs

1 teaspoon baking powder

Liberally grease a heart-shaped pan (the one I used is about 9 inches across at its widest point, and holds just over a quart of liquid). Preheat the oven to 350°F.

For the topping, beat the butter and sugar together, then spread it over the base of the cake pan—it will be a very thin layer, do not be alarmed. Then arrange the drained berries on top of the topping, in the most artistic way you can manage.

Make the cake by creaming the butter and sugar together, adding the eggs and the 2 tablespoons of reserved berry juice. Sift in the flour and baking powder and fold through.

Spread the cake batter over the berries, covering them, then bake for 35 minutes. Cool for 5 minutes on a wire rack, then, trying not to burn your fingers, turn the cake out onto a serving plate. It will look fantastic. The only thing about heart-shaped cakes is that they're tricky to cut into slices that don't look peculiar. I can see no way round it, I'm sorry. Serve warm or cold, it's up to you.

Pear, Almond, and Tahini Cake

Now *this* almost does count as healthy eating. It's dairy free—no butter or eggs—the fat is provided by the tahini. (I'm assuming you're familiar with tahini? It's a delicious paste made by crushing sesame seeds.) Also, this recipe has no sugar! I used date syrup, which I got in my local health food store, but if you have trouble getting hold of it, you can use another syrup, for example, maple syrup.

Serves 12–14

8 ounces tahini

9 ounces date syrup

1 teaspoon baking soda

1¾ cups all-purpose flour

1 teaspoon ground cinnamon

¾ cup almonds, chopped roughly

5 ounces pears, peeled and diced into ½-inch cubes*

1 cup apple juice**

* You can even use canned if you haven't any fresh ones handy. I did.

** If you've decided to use canned pears, you can use the leftover pear juice. If it doesn't come to quite 1 cup, top it off with apple juice.

Grease a 9-inch cake pan and line the base with parchment paper. Preheat the oven to 325°F.

Give the tahini a quick stir while it's still in its jar, because the oil usually separates into a layer on the top. Then pour into a mixing bowl and beat with the date syrup. Add the baking soda and mix again.

In a separate bowl, combine the sifted flour, cinnamon, almonds, and diced pears. Add a third of the flour/nut mixture to the tahini and mix. Add half the apple juice, then mix.

Add another third of the flour, then the other half of the juice. Finish with the remaining flour and mix until combined.

Pour the batter into the pan and bake for 45 minutes. After 30 minutes drop the oven temperature to 325°F and cover the cake loosely with aluminum foil for the final 10 minutes. Remove from the oven and let the cake cool in the pan. It is so rich and wonderful it doesn't need any sort of icing.

German Stollen Cake

This wonderful cake is traditionally served in Germany at Christmastime. It's fabulous, a sort of bread-like fruitcake, but with a hidden heart of marzipan. It involves the use of yeast, which used to scare the daylights out of me. Then I discovered dried instant yeast and it's changed my world.

I've read dozens of Stollen recipes, in the hope of making one as authentically German as possible, but there's such a wide variety of ingredients and methods that my head nearly exploded. I've experimented with a fair few versions, and in the end, I decided on this recipe because it's quite easy and phenomenally delicious.

Makes 2 smallish, 10-inch-long loaves, and you'll get about 10 slices out of each

⅓ cup currants
⅓ cup golden raisins
⅓ cup raisins
5 ounces glacé cherries, chopped
2 ounces candied citrus peel
4 tablespoons rum*
⅔ cup whole milk
2⅓ cups white bread flour
.25-ounce packet of active dry yeast
pinch of salt
5 tablespoons butter, at room temperature
1 egg
¼ cup superfine sugar
9 ounces marzipan**

To decorate
confectioners' sugar

* If you're not happy using alcohol, orange juice will do instead.

** A quick note on marzipan. Some people make their own and good luck to them. I bought mine at the supermarket.

Soak the fruit in the rum, cover, and set aside for at least a couple of hours. Overnight would be better.

When you're ready to start, heat the milk to lukewarm (no hotter or it'll kill the yeast) in a saucepan. In a separate bowl, sift the flour, the yeast, and the salt. Add the warm milk and mix well. You might see a few bubbles. This is an excellent sign, evidence that the yeast is working.

Add the butter, egg, and sugar and mix again. Cover the bowl with a damp, warm cloth and put in a warm place for about an hour and a half. You are leaving it to "proof"—this is a bread-making term, which means the yeast will do its magic and when you come back, the dough should have increased in volume, it might even have doubled, and will have developed a strange, elastic texture.

Turn the lump of dough (it will be quite sticky) out onto a floured work surface and "knock it back." This is *another* bread-making term, which means, basically, that you punch all the air out of it and reduce it to its original size. Then put it back into the bowl, add in the soaked fruit, and mix well.

If you're lucky enough to have a KitchenAid, use your dough hook to do the hard work and take a moment to give thanks. If you don't have a mixer, knead by hand on a well-floured surface for a good 5 minutes (sorry). At this point, line a baking sheet with parchment paper.

Take your marzipan, divide it in half and roll into two "ropes," each about 8 inches long. Take about half of the stollen dough out of the bowl. Place it on the floured surface and, using your hands, shape into a loaf about 9 inches long and 3½ inches across. Place the marzipan rope down along the length of the loaf, in the middle, then fold in the sides of the stollen dough and squeeze them together so that

•••

the marzipan is completely covered. Transfer the loaf to your prepared baking sheet, seam side down.

Repeat the process for the second loaf, then cover the two loaves with a damp, warm cloth and leave to proof—yes, again—for about 40 minutes. (*Entre nous*, my loaves don't puff out and rise at all during this second "proofing," but still taste lovely. I don't know what to make of it.)

Preheat the oven to 350°F and bake the loaves for 10 minutes. Then lower the temperature to 300°F and bake for another 30 to 40 minutes, until the loaves look golden brown. Remove them from the baking sheet, cool on a wire rack, and sprinkle with confectioners' sugar. (Do it through a sieve for a nice, even effect.)

Corn, Coconut, and Lime Loaf

Corn. Yes, I know, strange for a cake. But the clue is in the name it also goes by. *Sweet* corn. Not *savory* corn. Or *sour* corn. *Sweet* corn. I had to fiddle around with this recipe a lot because even though it was delicious and sweet and texturally very interesting, it wouldn't rise. After a fair bit of experimentation, I concluded that the heaviness of the corn was responsible and I was in despair, my amigos, *despair*. I thought I'd just have to let this one go. Then, in a lightbulb moment, I hit on the notion of separating the eggs and beating the whites into a light, airy cloud, then I let the battle commence. I pitted the corn against the beaten egg whites in a bare-knuckle fight—heaviness versus lightness. And guess what? Everyone's a winner!

Makes 12 slices

9 tablespoons butter

½ cup superfine sugar

3 eggs, separated

2 ounces dried coconut

3½ ounces canned corn, drained

zest of 2 limes

1 cup self-rising flour

1 teaspoon baking powder

1 teaspoon baking soda

Grease and line an 8 x 4 x 2½ inch loaf pan (or use a silicone one, much easier) and preheat the oven to 375°F.

Cream the butter and sugar until the mixture goes pale. Add the egg yolks, dried coconut, corn kernels, and lime zest and mix thoroughly. Sift in the flour, baking powder, and baking soda and fold through.

In a separate bowl, whisk the egg whites until stiff then, using a large metal spoon, carefully fold into the other mixture.

Pile into your prepared pan and bake for approximately 30 minutes. Cool on a wire rack, then upend from the pan and cut into slices.

CHOCOLATE

Chocolate and Sour Cream Cake

Chestnut and Rum Brownies

Ultimate Chocolate Brownies

Sean's Rosemary Truffles

Rocky Road Cake

Black Forest Gateau Trifle

Balsamic, Black Pepper, and Chocolate Cake

Quick-and-Easy Chocolate Fudge Pudding

Chocolate, Chili, and Cardamom Tart

Individual Chocolate Lava Cakes

Only an idiot would write a bakery book and not have a section on **CHOCOLATE**. That's all I can say. Therefore this chapter needs no introduction.

Chocolate and Sour Cream Cake

This is an excellent cake, very moist—thanks to the raspberries, I think—and surprisingly easy to make. Also, by using just raspberry jam to decorate, it keeps things very simple, if simple is what you're in the humor for.

Serves 12

3½ ounces dark chocolate (70% cocoa solids)

2 cups self-rising flour

1 teaspoon baking soda

1 teaspoon salt

1 cup superfine sugar

½ cup sunflower oil

1 cup sour cream

2 eggs, beaten

1 teaspoon vanilla extract

2 10-ounce cans of raspberries, drained of their juices*

To decorate

4–5 tablespoons raspberry jam

*Or approx. 8 ounces fresh raspberries, but—perhaps unexpectedly—I think the canned ones are better in this case. Their pulpiness, which in the real world might be seen as a bad thing, works very well for this cake.

Grease two 9-inch pans (you can use your hands or a paper towel) and preheat the oven to 350°F.

Melt the chocolate using your preferred method (see page 20) and leave to cool slightly.

Sift the flour and baking soda into a large mixing bowl. Add the salt and sugar, then stir in the oil and sour cream.

Mix in the melted chocolate.

Add in the beaten eggs, vanilla extract, and ¼ cup hot water. Finally, stir through the raspberries.

Divide the mixture between the two pans and bake for 25 minutes. Remove from the oven and set the pans on wire racks. Wait until the cakes are fully cooled before removing from their pans.

Sandwich the two layers together with raspberry jam.

Chestnut and Rum Brownies

Strange things, chestnuts, I find. Because, no matter how much bragging they do in their name, they don't *act* like nuts. Where's the crunch? Okay, *technically* they might be nuts, but texture-wise it's all a little unsettling. If I might speak frankly, they've a touch of the chickpea about them. But, handled right, they can be delicious.

There's both chestnut puree and actual chestnuts in this recipe, and I hope you don't have trouble getting the chestnut puree—it comes in cans if that's any help.

I've used milk chocolate here and it gives a slightly milder, sweeter taste than the dark chocolate in the Ultimate Chocolate Brownies recipe. But overall, it's still very, very, very rich. It's really okay to cut this into sixteen pieces because even a small piece is very effective.

Finally, feel free to use real rum if you'd prefer it to the rum extract, but if you're doing that, put in 2 tablespoons instead of 2 capfuls.

Serves 9 or 16, depending on how generous you want to be

7 ounces milk chocolate

7 tablespoons butter

2 eggs

1 egg yolk

1 cup light brown sugar

7 ounces chestnut puree

1 teaspoon vanilla extract

2 capfuls of rum extract

1½ cups all-purpose flour

½ teaspoon baking powder

3½ ounces chestnuts, roughly chopped

Liberally butter an 8-inch square pan (loose-bottomed, if possible) and preheat the oven to 350°F.

Melt the chocolate and butter together in a heatproof bowl over a saucepan of hot water.

In a separate bowl, beat the eggs, egg yolk, and sugar together, then add the melted chocolate and butter.

Add the chestnut puree, the vanilla extract, and the rum extract and mix well.

Sift in the flour and baking powder and fold through.

Stir in the chestnuts until they're evenly distributed.

Pour the brownie mixture into the prepared pan.

Bake for 30 minutes. It might look done on the top, but it won't be in the middle. Remember, this is a brownie, not a cake. Normal cake rules do not apply. Forget your Skewer Test! It has no place here.

Cool on a wire rack and leave for a long, long, long time (preferably overnight) before you cut it. It will be fabulously gooey and rich and wonderful.

Ultimate Chocolate Brownies

Yes, a second Brownies recipe! But this is quite different from the Chestnut and Rum Brownies—a lot darker. Very gooey, dense, sticky, chocolatey, wonderful.

Serves 9

8 ounces dark chocolate (70% cocoa solids), roughly chopped

1 cup (2 sticks) butter

2 eggs

2 egg yolks

1 cup light brown sugar

1½ cups all-purpose flour

½ teaspoon baking powder

pinch of salt

3½ ounces Brazil nuts, chopped quite small

Liberally butter an 8-inch square pan (loose-bottomed, if possible) and preheat the oven to 325°F.

Gently melt the chocolate and the butter together in a heatproof bowl over a pan of hot water.

Beat the eggs, egg yolks, and sugar together until they start to look a bit like caramel.

Pour in the melted chocolate and butter and mix together, but don't overbeat because if you do (I did on my first go) it sort of "coagulates." Not good.

Sift in the flour, baking powder, and salt and fold through.

Add the chopped Brazil nuts and gently mix.

Pour into the prepared pan and bake for a mere 20 minutes. As with the Chestnut and Rum Brownies, normal cake rules don't apply here. We are in a strange foreign land where your trusty Skewer Test has no place.

Put the pan on a wire rack to cool for at least 3 hours. If you cut it too soon, the brownie will leak all over the place. (I make these mistakes so that you don't have to…) When the time is up, turn out of the pan and cut into nine equal-sized squares.

FYI, and this can be our little secret, the square in the middle will be the most delicious of them all. I'm only saying, for when you're dishing them out, if you wanted to single someone out for a special treat—and who's to say it can't be you?—then the middle one is the very, very best.

Sean's Rosemary Truffles

Sean is my sister Caitriona's husband and is one of the best cooks in the whole wide world. He is a genius. Fact. These truffles are an adaptation—an homage, if you will—of some chocolate rosemary ice cream he once made me. Eating that dessert was one of the most agonizing experiences I have ever had because I knew that at some stage it would end. I knew that the time would come when I had eaten my last mouthful and there would be no more, and frankly I didn't know how I would carry on.

The ice cream was—no word of a lie—amazing and I wanted to try—humbly, humbly, of course—to re-create Sean's recipe. However, I didn't have an ice-cream maker so he suggested that, using the same basic ingredients, I make truffles instead. At first, this bamboozled me. "Truffles?" I asked. "Do you mean like the ones you get in a box? For your birthday? From an expensive chocolate shop?" "The very ones," he replied.

This was a complete revelation, that a person could make truffles in their own home. It was sort of like learning that I could knock up a pair of Christian Louboutin shoes in my utility room.

The ingredients are simple. The technique isn't too tricky either—I use a melon baller to make the roundy shapes. To decorate, I rolled the truffles in colored sanding sugar, which added color but no extra flavor. However, you could roll them in cocoa powder, dried coconut, ground pistachios, anything at all, which will, of course, change and enhance the flavor.

It's not necessary, but if you can get your hands on some mini paper liners to serve your truffles in, they will look extra beautiful.

Makes approx. 30–40

⅔ cup heavy cream
8 sprigs of fresh rosemary
5 ounces dark chocolate
  (70% cocoa solids)
2 tablespoons butter

To decorate
colored sanding sugar

Pour the cream into a saucepan.

Wash and dry the rosemary sprigs, then put 4 sprigs in the saucepan with the cream. Scald the cream (see page 21).

Remove the pan from the heat and let the rosemary flavor infuse the cream for about an hour.

Meanwhile, chop the chocolate very finely—use a food processor if it makes it easier—and place in a heatproof bowl. Dice the butter and add it to the chocolate.

Reheat the cream, then pour it through a sieve into the bowl of chocolate and butter. Discard the used rosemary sprigs.

Hopefully the heat of the cream will melt the chocolate and butter, but if it doesn't, please don't worry. Simply place the bowl over a saucepan of simmering water until everything is melted. Stir well to combine, remove from the heat, then lay the remaining 4 sprigs of rosemary along the surface. Don't immerse them deep in the mix because they are "the very devil" (love that phrase) to remove—sprigs coming off, defiantly refusing to leave and all sorts of difficulties.

•••

Refrigerate for several hours, even overnight, if you like. The mixture will set, but not become rock hard.

When you're ready to start making your truffles, take the mixture out of the fridge (you may need to let it warm a little before shaping), carefully peel off the sprigs of rosemary, and discard them.

Pour colored sanding sugar into a bowl.

Use your melon baller to scoop out a ball of the truffle mixture, then drop it into the bowl of sanding sugar and roll it around a little until it's coated. Place it in a mini paper liner. This will get easier with practice.

If you want, you can use the palms of your hands to encourage the truffles into roundy shapes, but bear in mind that this mixture melts and gets messy very quickly and the heat of your hands might just accelerate the process.

Indeed, even without using your hands, you might need to put the chocolate mixture back in the fridge periodically to firm it up again. But that's okay. Use the time in between to think pleasant thoughts. Like how impressed everyone will be when you present them with homemade truffles.

Rocky Road Cake

A no-bake cake. Easy peasy to make and everyone loves it.

Makes 16 squares

1 pound rich tea biscuits

10½ ounces dark chocolate (70% cocoa solids)

10½ ounces milk chocolate

14 tablespoons (1¾ sticks) butter

10½ ounces golden syrup (or substitute dark corn syrup)

3½ ounces dried dates, chopped small

3½ ounces dried apricots, chopped small

1 cup hazelnuts, skins off, roasted and chopped roughly

2 cups mini marshmallows

I used ready-roasted hazelnuts with their skins off, but if you prefer to roast your own: place the hazelnuts in a single layer on a baking sheet and roast in a 350°F oven for 5 to 8 minutes or under the broiler for 2 minutes until browned, checking regularly that they aren't burning.

To make the cake, begin by lining an 8-inch square pan with plastic wrap, leaving bits overhanging the sides so you can lift the cake out easily.

Break the biscuits into small pieces, smaller than bite-sized, but not reduced entirely to crumbs.

Melt the chocolate, butter, and golden syrup in a large heatproof bowl set over a pan of simmering water.

Remove the bowl from the heat and stir in the broken biscuits, then add the dried fruit, nuts, and marshmallows.

Stir well, then pour into the prepared pan and refrigerate for 6 hours.

Lift out of the pan and peel off the plastic wrap. Cut into sixteen chunks. Watch people devour.

Black Forest Gateau Trifle

This is a variation on an old favorite, "Ordinary Trifle." Are you familiar with "Ordinary Trifle"? Just in case you're not, it's a dessert traditionally made up of layers of strawberries, vanilla sponge, strawberry gelatin, custard, whipped cream, and more strawberries. But in keeping with the Black Forest theme, I'm using cherries, cherry gelatin, chocolate sponge, and chocolate custard.

The actual preparation time is short, but there are long, long, long gaps between each stage. It's best if you start on this the day before you plan on eating it.

Serves 8

2 1-pound cans of cherries, in syrup or juice—either is fine

2 3-ounce boxes of cherry gelatin

7 ounces chocolate sponge*

For the custard

6 egg yolks

⅔ cup superfine sugar

2 cups heavy cream

7 ounces dark chocolate (70% cocoa solids), chopped very finely

For the topping

⅔ cup heavy cream

*Or you could just buy a couple of chocolate muffins.

Drain one of the cans of cherries and set the juice aside, perhaps on the windowsill, it's up to you really. Put the cherries in the bottom of a 2-quart bowl, preferably see-through, so that people can see your layers and admire them. Pack them down tight.

Make the gelatin by dissolving it in a half cup boiling water in a heatproof pitcher. Use the leftover juice to make it up to a half quart, then leave until it's *almost* set. *Almost* set, but not *fully* set. A fine line, but an important one. This will take hours and hours and hours. Longer if you're in a hurry. But bank on at least 3 hours.

When the gelatin finally becomes thick and viscous, break the chocolate sponge into bite-sized pieces and put them into the bowl, on top of the cherries. Pour the gelatin in on top. More setting will take place.

Meanwhile, make a start on the chocolate custard. In an entirely new and separate bowl, whisk the egg yolks with the sugar until thick and foamy. In a saucepan scald the cream (see page 21).

Add half a cup of the scalded cream to the egg yolks, whisking continuously. When it's fully incorporated, add another half cup and so on until all the cream is in.

Keep whisking and the mixture should thicken somewhat, then add in the chopped chocolate and stir until it's melted.

Set aside to cool fully. And when I say "fully," I mean "fully" because if you pour the custard in on top of the gelatin when it's still even a little bit hot, it will melt the gelatin and the whole thing will be a shambles. A shambles, I tell you. (Christ, now that I think about it, making trifle has been one of the most stressful events of my life…)

So, yes, pour the fully cooled custard on top of the gelatin and leave aside to set—at least an hour.

Just before serving, whip the cream and spread it over the chocolate custard. Drain the second can of cherries—you can do what you like with the juice this time—and dot the cherries over the cream so that it looks like something out of a cartoon.

Balsamic, Black Pepper, and Chocolate Cake

This is an adaptation of a recipe from the (very divine!) *Divine Chocolate* recipe book. I came across it when I was just back from a family holiday in Tuscany and was jonesing for some Italian produce.

This is a handy little cake because it's egg- and dairy-free and astonishingly easy to make. Please don't be scared off by the balsamic syrup and black pepper—they give an interesting and slightly odd undertow but don't overpower things. However, I suggest serving this cake with mascarpone cheese and (this is where I might lose you) fresh basil and balsamic syrup. Think of sunny days in Italy is all I can say, and be grateful that at least I'm not advocating anchovies.

Serves 9, or 16 if you're feeling a bit mingy

1½ cups all-purpose flour
1 teaspoon baking powder
½ cup cocoa powder
1 cup light brown sugar
pinch of salt
½ teaspoon freshly ground
  black pepper
½ cup walnut oil
1 tablespoon balsamic syrup
1 teaspoon white wine
  vinegar

To serve

8-ounce tub of mascarpone
  cheese
a handful of finely torn fresh
  basil leaves*
a squeeze of balsamic syrup

*Go on! Go mad!

Grease a loose-bottomed 8-inch square cake pan and preheat the oven to 350°F.

Sift the flour, baking powder, and cocoa powder into a large mixing bowl. Add the sugar, salt, and black pepper.

Stir in the oil, balsamic syrup, white wine vinegar, and ⅔ cup warm water and mix well.

Pour into the pan and bake for about 30 minutes.

Please note: this will be quite a "flat" cake. It won't rise lots and there's only one layer. By itself, it won't look that impressive. I'm telling you now, so that you won't be disappointed. And so that you'll understand that what you serve it with is almost as important as the cake itself.

Cool on a wire rack.

When it has cooled, remove from the pan and cut into nine squares. Or sixteen.

Serve with a dollop of mascarpone cheese. And the basil leaves and balsamic syrup, if you're feeling daring, but if you're not, don't worry, it will still be wonderful.

Quick-and-Easy
Chocolate Fudge Pudding

This has an awful lot going for it, not least the fact that the chocolate taste is created by cocoa powder and not by chocolate itself, so there's a chance that there might be some cocoa powder in the house, unlike actual chocolate, which does not survive my regular "sweeps" (I mean, I eat it). Also, everything goes in together, at the same time—the sponge, the sauce, the lot. You just fling it in and forget about it for 40 minutes.

And it tastes great. The sponge is light and chocolatey and the sauce is gooey and fudgey. Just one thing about the size of the dish you use. Make sure it has a capacity of at least 1.5 quarts and is about 2 inches deep. This might seem big and deep, but the first couple of times I made this pudding, I used a 1-quart dish and the topping "burst its banks" and spattered itself over the inside of the oven. Poor Himself had a terrible job cleaning up after it.

Serves 6

For the sponge
½ cup light brown sugar
½ cup (1 stick) unsalted butter, at room temperature
1 teaspoon vanilla extract
2 eggs, lightly beaten
⅔ cup self-rising flour
⅓ cup cocoa powder
pinch of salt

For the sauce
½ cup dark brown sugar
⅓ cup cocoa powder
1 cup milk

Butter a 1.5-quart ovenproof dish. Preheat the oven to 350°F.

Cream together the sugar and butter until light and fluffy.

Beat in the vanilla extract and the eggs.

Sift in the flour, cocoa powder, and salt and fold through.

Spoon into the buttered ovenproof dish.

For the sauce, simply mix the sugar and the cocoa powder together and gradually whisk in the milk.

Pour evenly over the uncooked cake mixture—yes, I know it sounds odd, but it works.

Cover the dish loosely with a sheet of aluminum foil and bake for about 45 minutes.

Serve hot, warm, or cold, with or without cream.

Chocolate, Chili, and Cardamom Tart

This adaptation of a Lucas Hollweg recipe sounds—and tastes—very exotic, but is surprisingly easy to make. Especially because I'm giving you the super-easy option and encouraging you to use a store-bought shortcrust pastry shell. An 8-inch would be ideal, and it needs to be only ½ inch or ¾ inch deep. But if you'd prefer to make your own pastry, see the recipes in the Pastry chapter (page 112).

I've just used one chili here, which gives a hint of heat, a mere *soupçon*, if you will. If you'd prefer it to be hotter, add another chili, even two. But leave out the seeds. Even though they're the hottest part of the chili, for some reason they just become burny and nasty in this recipe.

Serves 6–8

1 8-inch pre-baked
  shortcrust pastry shell

For the filling

1 red chili

9 cardamom pods

1 cup heavy cream

¼ cup suerfine sugar

9 ounces dark chocolate
  (70% cocoa solids),
  broken into small pieces

5 tablespoons butter, cut into
  small cubes

To decorate (optional)

edible gold leaf

For the filling, chop the chili finely and discard the seeds. Rough up the cardamom pods by whizzing them in a coffee grinder, or flattening them with the blade of a wide knife and then chopping them as though they have insulted your mother.

Put the cream, sugar, cardamom pods, and chopped chili into a saucepan and gently bring to a simmer. Stir and heat until the sugar has dissolved, but be careful not to burn it.

Turn off the heat and leave to infuse for about an hour.

After an hour, reheat the cream mixture until it's just simmering, then put the chocolate and butter in a heatproof bowl and strain the warm cream onto it through a sieve, leaving the cardamom and chili behind.

Hopefully the heat of the cream will melt the chocolate and butter, in which case, stir until the mixture is smooth and glossy.

However, sometimes when I've made this, the heat of the cream simply isn't enough to melt the chocolate. If that happens, don't panic. Simply put the bowl over a saucepan of simmering water and stir until the chocolate dissolves and the whole mixture thickens up.

Pour it into the pastry shell and decide whether you're serving this to six or eight people. Place a piece of edible gold leaf in the middle of each "slice." This is a fiddly business, as gold leaf is floaty and sticks to everything, including itself. You might have to use kitchen tweezers (which are exactly like ordinary tweezers, except they live in my kitchen and are only used on food).

Leave to cool for a few hours at room temperature. The combination of cream, chocolate, and butter will set into a beautiful, almost fudgey texture, so wonderful that when you serve this tart to others, you might be met with jealousy. Rise above it.

Individual Chocolate Lava Cakes

The effort-to-effect ratio of these cakes is stunningly low. They're unbelievably simple to make (so simple that it actually made me uneasy, it made me wonder what I was doing wrong), yet they look and taste like something you'd pay good money for in a French restaurant. Especially if you manage to get them out of the ramekins (I'll come to that). These lava cakes are, in essence, warm chocolate cakes with a liquid chocolate center. The idea is that you cut the cake open and the molten chocolate rushes out. You get to decide how liquid they are by the length of time you bake them for.

Serves 4

6 ounces chocolate
  (70% cocoa solids)
¾ cup (1½ sticks) butter, cut
  into cubes
3 eggs
⅓ cup superfine sugar
⅔ cup all-purpose flour

To serve

thinly sliced strawberries
squirty cream or vanilla
  ice cream

Get four 8-ounce ramekins and butter the living daylights out of them. I really mean it. If you're planning on turning these little delights onto plates, the ramekins need to be larded with butter.

Preheat the oven to 350°F.

Melt the chocolate in a heatproof bowl over a saucepan of simmering water. Add the diced butter and stir until it melts.

In a separate bowl, beat the eggs and sugar until the mixture goes pale and foamy. Stir in the melted chocolate.

Sift in the flour and fold it through.

Divide the chocolate batter equally among the four buttered ramekins.

Cook for about 10 minutes if you want the cakes to be very runny; 12 minutes if you'd like them to be a little firmer. But I wouldn't leave them for much longer than 17 to 18 minutes.

At this stage, you can make life easy for yourself and simply sling the ramekins onto plates and throw on a dollop of vanilla ice cream. Or—painful gulp and squaring of shoulders—you could try taking the cakes out of the ramekins.

To do this, first stand the ramekins on a cold surface for about 5 minutes. The cakes will shrink a tiny bit—this is good, this gives you room to very carefully slide a small sharp knife in between the cake and the container.

Use the knife to gently loosen the connection between the two and when you feel you can do no more, tip a ramekin upside down onto a dessert plate, give it an encouraging little shake, and keep your fingers crossed that the cake will come out without a fight.

Even if it all goes a bit disastrous, with the base of the cake defiantly refusing to let go of the ramekin, remove it with a spoon, reattach it to the main body of the cake, and disguise the damage with a squirt of fake squirty cream or a dollop of vanilla ice cream.

Serve with thinly sliced strawberries and the aforementioned squirty cream or vanilla ice cream.

Index

Italics denote photographs

Lots of thank yous are in order here

I'd like to extend a huge thank you to the lovely Helen Cosgrove, who inspired me to make my first cake and who told me how to go about it. ("You need to buy a pan," she said.)

Thank you to everyone who contributed recipes: John Baines, Shirley Baines. Himself Baines, Sean Ferguson, Mam Keyes, Zaga Radojčić (and thank you Ljiljana Keyes for translating them from Serbian), Beth Nepomuceno, and Zeny Perez.

I did a couple of great day courses in baking at Cooks Academy in Dublin and I learned magical stuff about cake decoration in Cakes 4 Fun, Putney and the Cake Box, Dún Laoghaire. I'm very grateful for the expertise they shared with me.

The books and recipes of several famous bakers have inspired me and I'd like to give a special mention to the thrillingly innovative Dan Lepard, the lovely, lovely Nigel Slater, and, my very favorite, Catherine Leyden (check her out on Ireland AM).

Thank you to all the people I forced cake on and who gave me their opinion—too many to mention.

Thank you to all the people at Michael Joseph who embraced the idea for this book so enthusiastically and who worked on it—and with me!—with such diligence and patience: Lindsey Evans, Louise Moore, Liz Smith, Nick Lowndes, Lee Motley, John Hamilton, Sarah Fraser, and the copy editors. Thank you to Louisa Carter and the small army of people who "test-baked" all my recipes to make sure they worked. Thank you to my ever wonderful agent, Jonathan Lloyd, and all at Curtis Brown.

Thank you to Alistair Richardson for the beautiful photography, and to Barry McCall, his lovely assistant Paul, and my stalwart hair and makeup pal Tish Curry, for making the cover shot so painless.

Finally, the biggest thank you goes to Himself, who puts up with living in a house where everything is coated in a thin film of confectioners' sugar, and who photographed every single thing I baked and encouraged me every step of the way.

Available from Viking

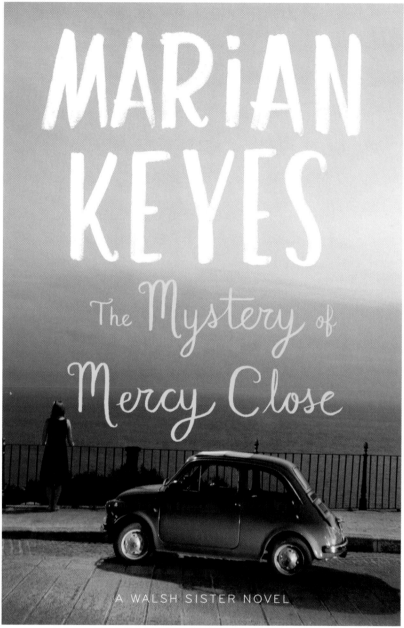

978-0-670-02524-4

Viking
An imprint of Penguin Group (USA) Inc.
www.penguin.com

VIKING

Also by Marian Keyes

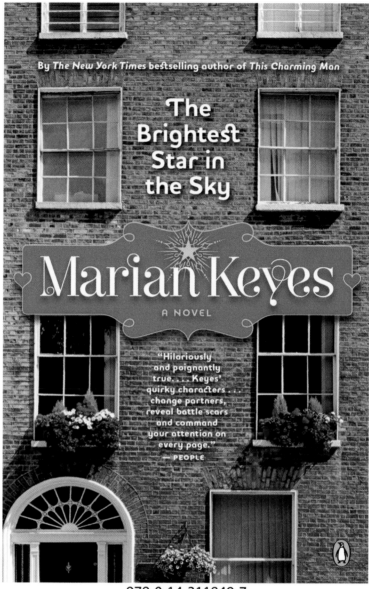

By *The New York Times* bestselling author of *This Charming Man*

The Brightest Star in the Sky

Marian Keyes

A NOVEL

"Hilariously and poignantly true. . . . Keyes' quirky characters . . . change partners, reveal battle scars and command your attention on every page."
—PEOPLE

978-0-14-311849-7

Available wherever books are sold